I   THE PRINT-LOVER

H. Daumier

Sir William Burrell

FRENCH PAINTING
And The
NINETEENTH CENTURY

By

JAMES LAVER

With Notes on Artists and Pictures by
MICHAEL SEVIER

and a Postscript by
ALFRED FLECHTHEIM

LONDON
B. T. BATSFORD LTD.
15 NORTH AUDLEY STREET, W.1

First Published September 1937

MADE AND PRINTED IN GREAT BRITAIN
TEXT BY T. & A. CONSTABLE LTD., EDINBURGH
PLATES BY JARROLD & SONS LTD., NORWICH

In Memory of
ALFRED FLECHTHEIM
Who died 9th March 1937
'*Marchand de Tableaux Créateur*'

PREFACE

MANY of the pictures illustrated in this volume were included in the memorable Exhibition of French Nineteenth-Century Painting organized by the Anglo-French Art and Travel Society at the New Burlington Galleries, London, in October 1936. The idea of the book first took shape during visits to this Exhibition, and its appearance in its present form would indeed have been impossible had it not been for the interest and help of the Organizing Committee, and in particular of Lord Ivor Spencer-Churchill, who provided invaluable facilities for photography and reproduction. The final choice of the illustrations, and much of the editorial work on the book, were undertaken by the late Alfred Flechtheim, whose enthusiasm was a stimulus to all concerned in its production. His recent death has robbed the world of art of one of its most vital and lovable personalities, and it is sad to feel that he did not live to see the fruits of the last of his many labours on behalf of the painters of the French nineteenth century.

The thanks of all concerned are also due to M. Paul Rosenberg, M. Georges Wildenstein, M. Félix Fénéon, M. Georges Duthuit, M. Paul Wallraf, M. Andry-Farcy, of the Musée de Grenoble, the Museum of Modern Art, of New York, and the Tooth and Leicester Galleries, of London, for many practical expressions of their interest, while general thanks are due to the owners of the pictures illustrated, or the galleries in which they hang, for the privilege of their inclusion. Finally, we must express our obligation to the Syndicat de la Propriété Artistique for the invariable kindness and courtesy shown towards us in smoothing out some of the more thorny ways of copyright.

B. T. BATSFORD LTD.

CONTENTS

2   LE BEC DU HOC, GRANDCAMP

G. Seurat

I

INTRODUCTION

THE nineteenth century is the century of easel-painting *par excellence*, and easel-painting is in the strict sense a monstrosity. It is a monstrosity in the sense that a prize carnation is a monstrosity, grown, not for the decoration of a house, or even for the adornment of a garden, but to make a sensation in a show. For it every other bloom on the stem has been sacrificed. It stands there alone, or hardly stands, for its head is so heavy that it needs an artificial prop to prevent it from breaking its stalk. A little earth still clings about its root, but how little! It can be picked up and carried about (though with infinite care) and can be ranged with others like itself in rows, by the horticultural equivalent of a hanging committee. Easel-painting is essentially a plant in a pot.

This may, of course, be an essential condition of the evolution of the Arts. The symphony only attains its full development when it is cut off from the theatre which gave it birth. Poetry only reveals its possibilities when it is no longer chanted, and attains its fullest complexity only when it is divorced altogether from the spoken voice. Painting is mere decoration until it has been divorced from architecture.

For the primitive mind painting is a grace added to the interior walls of a church; even the altar-piece painted on canvas is built into the structure of the altar, or hung so permanently above it that it no longer seems a separate thing. Divorced from sacred uses, its function is still to mingle with the architecture of the interior walls or ceilings of a palace, even at times to simulate such architectural decoration by a *trompe-l'œil*; it is something to add to the dignity of a Council Chamber, to dazzle the eyes of foreign Ambassadors, to reflect the glory of the Venetian Senate. Even when it ceases to be so public it is still thought of as an addition to the

A

amenities of a room, even if the room be only a rococo boudoir or the bed-room of a *femme galante*.

The change that took place at the beginning of the nineteenth century was no abrupt development. No doubt the forces which brought it about had long been in operation, but it was only then that the full consequences of their action became visible and their influence paramount.

The first of such causes was the decay of the patron; the Church, royal personages and great nobles had in turn been patrons of paintings, and however much they might differ in other particulars they had this in common, that they ordered pictures, and ordered them, very often, for specific purposes. In so doing they dictated to the artist the subject-matter, his style of treatment and very often the shape of wall he was expected to fill with his pictorial compositions. That this was no stunting slavery is attested by the quality of the works produced under such conditions. Such limitations, so far from hampering the artist, relieved him of half his burden, and most modern painters would be only too glad to accept such conditions if they were only to be found in the modern world. In that modern world the patron has been succeeded by the buyer who may or may not be forth-coming. In other words, the painter has to please the patron he has never met, whose taste, purposes and income are all equally unknown. The painter is free to take a canvas of whatever shape or size he thinks fit, to paint on it whatever he likes, in the manner of his own choosing. He then has to market his goods like a manufacturer, and if he cannot market them he must either live on charity or go out of business. In Art, as in so many other aspects of life, the change from status to contract produces a liberty which is largely an illusion.

The modern painter—that is, any painter living in an age in which the buyer has replaced the patron—finds that he is working more and more in a vacuum. For one thing, his art is divorced from the so-called minor arts —the very division into minor arts and *beaux-arts* is sufficient to prove it— and where in former ages he towered like a tree in undergrowth, now he stands like a tree in a park, naked about the roots. The decorative arts suffer perhaps most of all from this divorce and are never at a lower ebb of design and workmanship than in a great age of easel-painting; but the easel-painter suffers also, not only from the lack of a suitable frame for his work, but from a kind of spiritual isolation, for the Arts are ultimately one, with a common tradition, and when they are healthy, a unified development.

Another factor in the growing isolation of the artist was the collapse of the old system of apprenticeship which, in its turn, is part of the decay of the notion that the Arts were a kind of handicraft, more difficult perhaps than cabinet-making or jewellery, but of the same nature and needing the same kind of training. No doubt there has been something comparable to the modern Art School in former ages, as in the days of the Carracci at Bologna, and that too resulted inevitably in a kind of eclecticism. Such eclecticism is the curse of the Art School and inevitable from the mere nature of the teaching given. The rise of the Art Schools means the collapse of 'Schools of Art.' Raphael no longer learns his trade from Perugino. Instead he builds up his technique from every kind of painting at once; he may be taught by two masters with diametrically opposite notions of their craft, and it is left to him to choose, or rather to find, the manner which he is afterwards to practise. A great painter may have innumerable disciples or followers who are influenced by him, but they are influenced, not as a pupil is influenced by his master, but as a voter is influenced by a politician. It is no longer a matter of tuition; it is a matter of '*réclame*,' and this results on the one hand in a great ignorance of the technical processes of painting—on the technical side painting has never been so incompetent as it was in the early years of the nineteenth century— and on the other in an entirely new conception of the nature of the artist. The admired artist is no longer the master-craftsman, but the prophet. He paints no longer for the glory of God, or even for the glory of the Venetian Senate; he paints for his own glory, for the presentation of his own conception of the universe, for the promulgation of his own message.

This new notion of the artist as prophet was not confined to pictorial art, it was even more noticeable in the art of literature. Even a propagandist like Voltaire was a craftsman in the sense that he could construct a *Comédie-Ballet* as readily as he could write a satire against the Jesuits, and with the same sense of work well done. He might attack priests and kings, but it never occurred to him that the functions of the king, and the priest, and

3

the prophet as well, might be, and indeed should be, concentrated in the hands of the poets. The Artist as Genius—such is the new conception of poet and painter in the first half of the nineteenth century. This leads in turn to the conception of the artist as a rebel and an eccentric, but a discussion of this will find its place more naturally in an account of the romantic painters. At the moment it is sufficient to note that Art and Literature are subject to the same impulses and seem to form part of the same movement.

It is fashionable nowadays to deny that Literature has any rightful part in the productions of the pictorial artist. To say that a painter is 'literary' is to say that he is a painter of small account. Ever since it became the accepted axiom of criticism that all the Arts should aspire to the condition of Music—a doubtful statement for most Arts and meaningless in some— Literature has been anathema to most writers on Art subjects. 'Every picture tells a story' has become the recognized hallmark of bad painting; as well it might be after the orgy of anecdote indulged in by the less competent painters of the nineteenth century. But the claim that Painting should have no intellectual content whatever has led both critics and the painters themselves to some strange conclusions. It has even led some writers to the extreme conclusion that 'Every sacrifice to representation is something stolen from Art,' and the logical conclusion from this is that there is no true painting between the extreme primitive and Cézanne.

A possible reply to this is that a great deal of canvas has been covered with paint during that period, and if it is not painting it is still an important part of our social history and worthy of study. But the writers who talk of a sacrifice to representation are in reality begging the whole question. It is only the bad artist who *sacrifices* to representation. Good artists find in it merely one of those limitations which prove in practice to be 'not chains but wings,' and as essential to the full development of their power as the thick walls of the boiler are essential to the steam-engine. For the last generation aesthetic critics have been pursuing the will-o'-the-wisp of pure Art, pure Painting, pure Poetry, etc., until the ideal poem has come to seem a meaningless pattern of words and the ideal painting a pattern of meaningless shapes. The pursuit of abstract Art has done good, no doubt, in

4

3   THE BATHERS

P. Cézanne

Lord Ivor Spencer-Churchill

freeing the artist from the tyranny of the photographic vision, but it is not, and cannot be, an end in itself. Nor has it succeeded in banishing Literature, if we may judge from the number of pamphlets necessary to explain the productions of abstract painters. It is perhaps natural enough that Literature should always have the last word.

Indeed there is no escape from Literature, for Literature is the Age thinking aloud. It is the reflection of its hopes, and fears, and aspirations, and a man can no more escape from Literature than a fish can escape from the water in which he swims. The mistake is to regard the pictorial artist as somehow not a man but a painter living all by himself under the glass shade of an air pump—or should it be in a padded cell? For to care nothing for representation is to care nothing for communication with the rest of mankind. It is to shut yourself up with a private language, to converse endlessly with yourself in terms unintelligible to the rest of the world, to provide in short the stock subject of investigation by the psycho-analyst and the alienist. It is not, perhaps, to be an artist.

Such extreme cases, however, scarcely need to be dealt with in a study of nineteenth-century painting. Few nineteenth-century painters would have made such extreme claims to independence, but they did claim to be independent of the Church, the Monarchy and the aristocratic patron, and to be able to paint to please themselves. What this means in practice is that, no longer sheltered by the specialized nature of their accepted function, they were open to every change of ideals, every fluctuation of taste and every wind of fashion. For painters are also men, and as men they are the children of their Age, even if more than most men they are sometimes the fathers of the Age-to-be. To believe this is not to fall into the error of Taine. The original artist is not the mere product of his environment. Genius is always a 'sport,' in the biological sense. A man is a genius because of his originality, and to believe in such originality is the only escape from a dead determinism. But even a genius is none the less a part of his Age, and his every action and even his every thought is conditioned by his epoch. He may seek, as the classical painters have done, to express his Age in its totality, to bring about a new synthesis, to form the world in the image of his own desires. Or he may strive, like the romantic painters, to escape from his Age, to

B

repudiate it altogether, but in doing so he merely expresses in his own work the universal escape-longings of his period. The original and recalcitrant geniuses often seem in retrospect to be the most representative of the period in which they live. And therefore it is impossible to study them in isolation, to say, 'Here is the man who painted this and that, but it is a matter of indifference to me what he thought and dreamed of, and what his contemporaries thought and dreamed of.' The history of Art cannot be explained in terms of technique. The present monograph, therefore, is an attempt to place the chief artists of the nineteenth century in their environment, to show the influences by which they were surrounded, the ideals they set themselves, the waking dream which occupied most of their thoughts. To do so with any completeness is obviously beyond the scope of such a volume, but it is hoped that at least some of the main streams may have been described, the main currents indicated and the principal reefs and shallows charted.

J. L. David

4   THE LUXEMBOURG GARDENS

Musée du Louvre, Paris

5   A YOUNG GIRL

J. L. David

Sir Philip Sassoon, Bart.

II

REPUBLICAN VIRTUE

In the pages which follow I have so far as possible avoided the words 'Classic' and 'Romantic.' So much ink has been spilt in an attempt to define them, or even to talk about them without defining them, that little purpose is served by continuing the controversy. Besides, no sooner has one attempted to separate into two camps Classical and Romantic painters than the most outstanding examples of each are seen to bristle with contradictions. Ingres, in his early days, was called 'a Gothic painter,' and it is recorded that Delacroix on being hailed by a fervent admirer as the Victor Hugo of painting, replied, 'Vous vous trompez, monsieur, je suis un pur classique.'

'N'est pas classique qui veux.' Even those who think they are most completely so have usually seized upon some inessentials of a former epoch, when life was supposed, in retrospect, to have been more unified or simple than now, and to have magnified these inessentials into doctrines. This was never more noticeable than at the end of the eighteenth century, when the French revolutionaries, having repudiated their own national traditions, looked round for another Age and another people on which they could model their conduct, with that thirst for continuity which is at least as active a desire of the human mind as the desire for change. It was none the less a delusion on the part of the members of the Convention that they bore any close resemblance to the Senators of Ancient Rome, either in ideas, programme or appearance. Such notions, however, are but the more potent for being illusions, and the closing years of the eighteenth century cannot be understood unless we are willing to take into account this almost universal background of the French mind. It was not Imperial Rome that they looked back to; it was Republican Rome—the Age of virtue, simplicity, frugality, order and justice. That such a Republican Rome ever existed may be only another delusion, but that does not alter the effects of the dream.

Men were tired of the extravagance and frivolity of the *ancien régime*.

They were tired of boudoir Art with its sugary sentimentality and its very real eroticism. Pictures, they considered, should no longer minister to private vices, but should promote public virtues, and to do this they must denude themselves of all those superficial attractions characteristic of eighteenth-century painters. All that revelling in flesh tints and voluptuous contours should be replaced by a new kind of art—cold, hard and linear—constructed with the rigidity of mathematics, founded on the Academic nude, and inclining the spectator to chaste emotions and public spirit. The fact that the heroes of Ancient Greece and Rome certainly did not perform their public functions in a state of complete nudity did not deter David and his followers for a moment. The Academic nude, harshly lit by the studio lamp, painted *in vacuo* without any enveloping atmosphere and transferred to the canvas as a flat shape, was too useful for the purposes they had in mind. They sought to impose a certain rigidity on the sprawling lines of the rococo tradition, and in this they were certainly successful.

Of course, the same influences had been at work in decoration for some years before the French Revolution broke out. Louis XVI furniture is nothing but such a stiffening of line, and in all details of the decorative art of the period the elements of the Empire styles are already laid down. Even in painting, David was not himself the pioneer; already, before the Revolution, Joseph Marie Vien had given more than a hint of the method which the greater man was afterwards to pursue to its logical conclusion.

But the tradition went back much further than that, and David's Revolution in one sense was merely an attempt to revive the Academic principles of the seventeenth century, when the *École de Rome* was founded. It even went back to the sixteenth, when the artists of the second Italian Renaissance came to France and founded an Academy under the protection of the Medici. By the time of Louis XVI the idea of an Academy to rule over the Arts seemed as natural as an Academy of Letters, and a rigid hierarchy was established outside of which there was no salvation, or at least no money and no public commissions. Such an Academy must, to justify its existence, enunciate principles, promulgate laws and strive to reduce the whole of painting to a science. It is bound to set up an eternal model of beauty, and, the circumstances being what they were, the model it chose was bound to be Greek or Romano-Greek.

From this it followed that beauty was a matter of proportion, and that such proportion could be scientifically determined by proper measurement of Greek statues; hence the preference for the idealized studio nude, and the theory that no deviation into expression should be permitted unless the Greeks had already shown the way, as in their dancing fauns or other monsters.

No doubt there was a certain value in such discipline, a value which the modern Age in its attempts to seize the deeper principles of classicism and to build up its own architectural system of painting, should be the last to condemn. A man like Poussin was able to turn the principles of the School to his own use with complete success. He adopted the classical subject, the rigid construction, the compositional repose and formal solidity of the classical ideals. In the hands of less gifted painters, however, such ideals degenerated into a mannerism, and it was quite plain as the seventeenth century turned into the eighteenth that whatever vitality the School had ever possessed was rapidly becoming exhausted. The best French painters were those who, whatever lip-service they might pay to Academic principles, went their own way; and towards the end of the century a great deal of French painting had trickled away to the two (psychologically) related streams of sensuality and sentimentality. David's reform was essentially a harking back to the earlier tradition, and that he was able to do this with success was not primarily due to his capacity as a painter, but to his sincerity as a man, for he believed in the classical tradition, even when he understood it imperfectly, and so he was able to revivify it, and present it to the world as almost a new discovery.

It is curious to reflect in this connection that his portraits show little or no trace of that obsession with proportion and arrangement which characterized his more ambitious canvases. Indeed there is in them a vividness and a realism which was later to be elevated into a doctrine and used to sweep away the very principles which he had most at heart. His portraits were consequently the only part of his work in which late nineteenth-century criticism saw any virtue whatever. It regarded his vast classical subject-pieces as empty and pretentious. The modern Age must give him at least the credit for striving, with whatever degree of success, to give painting its true place in the life of the community, to make it something more than mere illustration or idle amusement; to make it, in short, the ideal expression of the life of his time.

9

Louis David himself was one of the most remarkable men in the history of painting—remarkable not only for his absorption in his task but for the fact that he regarded his artistic activities as only a part of his public function. There was in him no rigid division between the man and the artist, and his painting of heroic scenes from the ancient world and his revolutionary activity are part of the same crusade. He had already painted the '*Le Serment des Horaces*' and the 'Paris and Helen' before the Revolution, but in the Salon of 1789 he exhibited his 'Brutus,' which formed a rallying point for Republican sentiment and established David at a stroke as the painter of the New Age. The Jacobins commissioned him to paint a Revolutionary picture, but what was perhaps more to the purpose, they gave him an official appointment which made him into a kind of Art Dictator. In this capacity his reforms, if they can be called so, were largely responsible for that transformation of the painting apprentice into the art student which has been discussed in the first chapter and of which the effects were to be so far-reaching.

The *Directoire* dethroned him for a time, but even during this period his influence was by no means negligible. His picture of the Sabine women, although not publicly exhibited, was known to all the art world of Paris, and visiting foreigners went to his studio to see it. As may well be imagined, the life of the men of the *Directoire* was little to David's taste, and he welcomed the advent of Napoleon with an enthusiasm which to some of his revolutionary friends seemed little short of treason to their common ideals. In reality it was not so. After all, what could be more Roman than an Emperor and one whose armies fought under the Eagles. Then, too, Napoleon embodied many of those ideals which had made David a revolutionary. It was 'Order' that the painter admired, even fanatically. He had approved the butchery of Robespierre because he thought it purified the State of undesirable elements. He admired Napoleon's strong-handed methods for the same reason. And he had less reason to be called a turncoat than the majority of his French contemporaries, for few of whom Revolution had appeared in the high moral light which made it admirable in the eyes of David. He saw nothing incompatible in painting propaganda pictures for Napoleon and representations in his old manner of the Spartans at Thermopylae at the same time.

6 NAPOLEON AS FIRST CONSUL

J. D. Ingres

Musée de Liège

7 PORTRAIT OF THE PRINCESSE DE BROGLIE

J. D. Ingres   *Duc de Broglie*

His most important pupils were Ingres, Gros and Gérard. Of these, Gros identified himself most completely with the Napoleonic propaganda and he was at one time attached to the Emperor's staff, but his manner was very far from being as rigidly classical as David's. He painted Napoleon and his Marshals in contemporary clothes, in dramatic attitudes, and he can be seen in retrospect to have been one of the founders of that most romantic conception, 'The Napoleonic Legend.' Gérard was more classical, both in manner and in subject-matter, but it was on Ingres, who seemed at first to be anti-classical, that the mantle of David ultimately fell.

Ingres is an extremely puzzling artist and his career is full of contradictions. It is customary for modern painters, enthusiastic for the classical tradition, and endeavouring to imbue painting with something of the dignity and solidity of architecture, to express the greatest admiration for Ingres. But it is doubtful if many of them have seen any of this painter's work except a few of his drawings and reproductions of the more celebrated classical subject-pieces. The drawings are indeed admirable; little miracles of caligraphic line and expressive contour; the linear tradition carried to its highest point of achievement. But nothing is less architectural than a caligraphic line, and it is this line which interested Ingres in all his pictures, from the early 'Jupiter and Thetis' to the very late '*Bain Turc*,' which has no other *raison d'être* than the artist's delight in a sinuous arabesque.

He was awarded a Prix de Rome at the very beginning of the Empire, and, had he been able to afford to accept it, his Napoleon pictures would probably never have been painted at all. In Italy he lived first in Rome, then in Florence, and proved himself susceptible not only to the charms of the antique, but to those of every other school of painting represented in the Italian collections.

His '*Grande Odalisque*' might have been painted by an Italianate Frenchman at the Court of Francis the First. His 'Francesca da Rimini' might have been painted by an English pre-Raphaelite. The restoration of the Bourbons had produced a taste for French historical pictures—a taste which was the foundation of the romantic movement that will be dealt with more fully in the next chapter. But Ingres was so well aware of this taste and apparently so much in sympathy with it that the pictures which he brought back with him to Paris in 1824 were almost all in what claimed to be called the '*Style Troubadour*.'

During his absence in Rome, however, a new school of French painting had arisen—a school so much more 'Troubadour' than himself, so revolutionary in its technique, so contemptuous of the suave outline which he adored, that almost in self-defence he found himself thrown back on the Davidian tradition, and it was he who was destined to continue it and to pass it on to the middle of the nineteenth century.

The contradictions of Ingres' art are, as it were, on the surface, and if they cannot be readily explained they can at least be plotted. Prud'hon is an even more puzzling figure; his subject-matter is predominantly classical in the sense that it deals with mythological themes, but his contours, instead of being the hard outlines of David, are bathed in the soft chiaroscuro of Correggio. He obtained a brief period of success under Napoleon—a success which diverted him from his chosen subjects to paint '*Le Triomphe de Bonaparte*'—but for the greater part of his life he lived in poverty, and it was only after his death that his pictures received the appreciation due to them. He had, in any case, less influence on subsequent paintings than either David or Ingres.

The influence of the two latter was immense and almost wholly deleterious. Between them they reinforced the power of the Academic tradition so strongly that only the most original painters could escape from it. Their love for the idealized nude became in the hands of their followers a lifeless convention of the worst kind. Even today it is not impossible, while walking through the endless galleries of the Paris Salon, to see some waxen female figure as airless as David's but without the underlying strength of his structure, as voluptuous as Ingres', but without any of the enchantment of his living line. During the whole course of the nineteenth century such paintings were produced by thousands, till the public grew so accustomed to the sight of what has been called '*La Femme de l'École*' that it refused to recognize that any other kind of nude was possible. '*La Femme de l'École*' was like no living woman that ever existed, yet with her majestic or simpering expression, her mathematically symmetrical busts, her unnaturally small hands and her skin conventionally pink, she was to be seen by dozens on the walls of every public exhibition of painting in Europe. And for this the pupils and imitators of Ingres must be held largely responsible. Signol, Duval and Delaroche—who can endure to look at their work today? Even those painters like Couture and Paul Baudry who had certain powers as draughtsmen or designers seem unendurably commonplace and empty. The only pupil of Ingres who has left us any work which can still be admired is Théodore Chassériau, who broke away from his master as soon as he could and acknowledged in his own practice the inspiration of Delacroix.

The ultimate degeneration of the Ingres impulse can be seen under the Second Empire in the work of men like Cabanel and Bouguereau, and it is a damning criticism of the Academic tradition that the works of this latter painter were accepted for many years by a large proportion of the French, and indeed of the European public, as the highest expression of painting. But it is unfair, perhaps, to judge any tradition by its ultimate derivative, and Ingres and David cannot be held responsible for the fate of the stream which, already muddied in the time of Couture, has lost itself in such a bog of meaningless incompetence. There is much in the work of both masters that a modern painter can use for his own inspiration; even if the architecture of David is not always as solid as it seems, and the line of Ingres sometimes more titillating than expressive.

At the end of the first quarter of the nineteenth century, however, the main stream of French painting lies elsewhere, and it is this which we must now consider. David had hoped not only to restore painting to a classical purity and simplicity, but to reintegrate the whole of life under the discipline of Republican virtue. How completely he failed in this needs no stressing. What the Revolution and Napoleon had been unable to accomplish, restored Bourbons were hardly likely even to attempt. The restoration of the *ancien régime* did not restore the ancient world. Instead there was the new world of the triumphant bourgeoisie and growing industrialism, and in the face of such a world the artist gave up all attempts at integration. He was content to escape. It is the nature of his escape which must be considered in the next two chapters.

C

13

8 "LA BELLE ZÉLIE"

J. D. Ingres   *Musée de Rouen*

9　THE YOUNG AMALRIC

Baron Gros

M. Roger Cambon

NOTES ON ARTISTS AND PICTURES

DAVID, JACQUES-LOUIS
1748–1825

Louis David, who was the son of a draper, was born in Paris in 1748. He became the pupil of the historical painter, Viau, whom he accompanied to Rome, where his classical ideals developed and matured. He returned to Paris in 1780 and married Mlle. Pécoul, a wealthy heiress. When the Revolution broke out he flung himself passionately into political life, and as a deputy to the Convention was one of those who signed the death decree of Louis XVI. For two years he retained a powerful position in the revolutionary government and was to all intents and purposes dictator of the arts. But after the fall of Robespierre in 1794 he became suspect, and was twice incarcerated in the Luxembourg, which then served as a prison. After his final release he took no more part in politics and lived in a studio which the Directorate gave him in the rue de Seine, where he held a public exhibition of his favourite picture 'Les Sabines' (Louvre)—an exhibition which lasted five years and brought in over 60,000 francs in gate-money. When Napoleon, whom David first met in 1798, became Emperor, he nominated him *Premier Peintre de l'Empereur*. In that capacity David produced the series of paintings which forms a pictorial epic devoted to the glorification of Napoleon, and includes the famous 'La Distribution des Aigles' (Versailles) and 'Le Sacre de Napoléon' (Louvre). These canvases were so huge that studios were too small to hold them, and the artist was given the church of Cluny to work in. With the fall of the Empire David's star declined, and in 1818 he had to take refuge in Brussels, where he died in 1825.

4. THE LUXEMBOURG GARDENS.
> Oil on canvas, 21⅜×25 inches.
> Painted towards the end of the eighteenth century as a memento of the time

when the artist was kept a prisoner in the Luxembourg, and when his children used to come and play in the garden which his windows overlooked. The picture was given by David to his friend Seriziat. It is the only landscape he ever painted. Formerly in the possession of Sosthène Moreau. Bought and presented to the Museum by MM. Bernheim jeunes in 1912.

Coll.: *Musée du Louvre, Paris.*

5. A YOUNG GIRL.

Oil on canvas, 29 × 18½ inches.

Coll.: *Rt. Hon. Sir Philip Sassoon, Bart., M.P., London.*

INGRES, JEAN-AUGUSTE-DOMINIQUE
1780–1867

Ingres, whose father was a sculptor and miniature painter, was born at Montauban in 1780. When he came to Paris to study with David, young Ingres earned his living as a violinist in a theatre on the Boulevards. When twenty-one he was awarded the Prix de Rome, and shortly afterwards was commissioned to paint 'Bonaparte as First Consul' (Liège) and 'Napoleon as Emperor' (Invalides). In 1806 he went to Italy and stayed fourteen years in Rome and four in Florence. In Rome he met and married a young woman who, like himself, was a native of Montauban. On his return to Paris in 1824 he exhibited at the Salon 'Le Vœu de Louis XIII' (Montauban Cathedral), was made a member of the Institute and received the Legion of Honour. He became the leader of the Classical School and the irreconcilable opponent of Delacroix and the Romantics, against whose 'troubadour' manner of painting he directed his famous maxim, '*Le dessin est la probité de l'art.*'

In 1834 he once more went to Italy, having been appointed director of the French Academy in Rome. He remained in Rome until 1841, when he returned to Paris, where he spent the rest of his life. He amassed many honours, was promoted Grand Officer of the Legion of Honour and became a senator. His end came in 1867 when he was eighty-seven. A week before he died he was still at work.

6. NAPOLEON AS FIRST CONSUL.

Oil on canvas, 89 × 56¾ inches.

Commissioned by the First Consul in July 1803 for presentation to the town of Liège to commemorate the reconstruction of the Faubourg d'Amercœur. The newly erected church is seen through the window. Napoleon refused to sit for the portrait and Ingres was only once permitted to 'have a look' at him at Saint-Cloud.

Signed: *Ingres*, and dated: *ANXII* (1805).

Coll.: *Musée de Liège*.

7. PORTRAIT OF THE PRINCESSE DE BROGLIE.

Oil on canvas, $70\frac{3}{4} \times 39\frac{1}{4}$ inches.

The portrait was begun in 1851 and finished two years later.

Signed: *J. Ingres*, and dated: *1853*.

Coll.: *Duc de Broglie, Paris*.

8. 'LA BELLE ZÉLIE.'

Oil on canvas, $23\frac{1}{4} \times 19\frac{1}{4}$ inches.

A portrait of Mme. Aymon.

Signed: *Ingres*, and dated: *1806*.

Former collections: Eudoxe Marcille; Jacques Reiset; Féral Cussac. Acquired by the Museum in 1870.

Coll.: *Musée de Rouen*.

14. VENUS WOUNDED BY DIOMEDES.

Oil on panel, $10\frac{1}{4} \times 12\frac{1}{2}$ inches.

Signed: *J. Ingres*.

Formerly in the collection of Mme. L'Hériller, Paris.

Coll.: *Baron Robert von Hirsch, Basle*.

GROS, ANTOINE-JEAN, BARON
1771–1835

The son of a miniature painter, Antoine-Jean Gros was born in Paris in 1771 and became a pupil of David in 1785. In 1793 he went to Italy as an official artist attached to Napoleon's armies. In 1801 he produced 'Bonaparte au Pont d'Arcole' (Versailles), which was followed by other works commemorating Napoleon's victories. He was highly appreciated by Napoleon, who decorated him and appointed him member of the committee which had to select the works of art that the conquered Italian cities had to cede to France. Gros continued to enjoy royal patronage under the Bourbons and was created a Baron by Charles X. But the violent attacks continually made against him by the partisans of the Romantic School preyed upon his mind, and in 1835, after making the remark that 'there is but one misfortune for which art provides no remedy and that is the survival of one's self,' he committed suicide by throwing himself into the Seine, near Meudon.

9. THE YOUNG AMALRIC.

Oil on canvas, 18×15 inches.
Portrait of Jacques Amalric, a nephew of the artist.
Signed and dated 1804.
Formerly in the possession of M. Cresté, a nephew of Mme. Jacques Amalric.
Coll.: *M. Roger Cambon, France.*

GÉRARD, FRANÇOIS-PASCAL-SIMON, BARON
1770–1837

Gérard was the son of a servant in the employ of the French Ambassador in Rome, and was born in that city in 1770. In 1782 he came with his parents to Paris, where soon afterwards he became the pupil of the sculptor Pajou, with whom he stayed for two years. Later he joined the studio of Brenet and in 1786 that of David. In 1792, owing to the latter's influence, he became a member of the Revolutionary Tribunal and was for three years more active as a politician than as a painter. In 1795 he produced his 'Bélisaire' (Munich) and in 1798 'Amour et Psyché' (Louvre). Napoleon commissioned him to paint numerous official portraits, and Louis XVIII, Charles X and Louis-Philippe all extended him their patronage. Gérard was one of the original Knights of the Legion of Honour, became a member of the Institute in 1812 and was made a Baron in 1819. He died in Paris in 1837.

10. PORTRAIT OF JOACHIM MURAT.

Oil on canvas.
Coll.: *Musée de Versailles.*

PRUD'HON, PIERRE-PAUL
1758–1823

Prud'hon, who was the thirteenth child of a stonemason, was born in 1758 at Cluny, where he was brought up by the monks of the Abbey.

10 PORTRAIT OF JOACHIM MURAT

Baron Gérard

Musée de Versailles

11 THE HAPPY MOTHER

P. P. Prud'hon

The Wallace Collection, London

He received his artistic tuition first from Devosge at Dijon and then from Wille in Paris. In 1781 he went to Rome and remained in Italy for six years, studying the old masters and being especially attracted by Leonardo and Correggio, who distinctly influenced his style. On his return to Paris he lived the life of a struggling artist until the First Empire, when the change in public taste brought him popularity and he became a favourite with the two Empresses. He executed decorations for various public and private buildings, and in 1808 received the Legion of Honour for his two paintings, 'Crime pursued by Vengeance and Justice' and 'Psyche carried off by Zephyrs,' both of which are in the Louvre. In 1816 he was elected a member of the Institute.

Prud'hon's married life was unhappy, but later he found consolation in the devoted companionship of his pupil, Constance Mayer (1778-1821), who had become his mistress. Their union ended abruptly by Constance Mayer committing suicide in 1821. Prud'hon died in Paris two years later—in 1823.

11. THE HAPPY MOTHER.

Oil on canvas, $9\frac{1}{8} \times 6\frac{5}{8}$ inches.

Constance Mayer painted from this sketch the life-size 'La Mère Heureuse' which is in the Louvre.

Bought by Lord Hertford in 1846 from De Saint in Paris for 3150 francs.

Coll.: *The Wallace Collection, London.*

GIRODET DE ROUCY TRIOSON, ANNE-LOUIS

1767–1824

Girodet was born at Montargis in 1767 and, becoming an orphan in childhood, was adopted by his guardian, M. Trioson, whose name he later added to his own. In 1785 he joined the studio of David and became his favourite pupil. In 1789 he was awarded the Prix de Rome and went to Italy, returning to Paris in 1798. In 1812 his adopted father died, leaving him a considerable fortune. From then on Girodet, who was never a prolific worker, gave up painting altogether and devoted his time to literary pursuits and to the building of houses. He died in Paris in 1824.

12. MADEMOISELLE LANGE AS DANAË.

Oil on canvas, 24 × 19¼ inches.

In 1799 Girodet painted a portrait of Mlle. Lange, the actress. She did not approve of it, and when her criticisms were reported to the artist, in a rage he cut the canvas to pieces and sent the débris to the sitter. Then, as a revenge, he painted the present picture, in which Mlle. Lange is represented as Danaë, whilst the traits of her lover are caricatured in the head of the turkey on the left. The painting was exhibited at the Salon, but caused such a scandal that it had to be withdrawn after a few days.

Formerly in the collection of M. Raoul Brinquant.

Coll.: *M. Georges Wildenstein, Paris.*

12 MADEMOISELLE LANGE AS DANAË

L. Girodet

M. Georges Wildenstein

13 SLAVES HOLDING A HORSE

T. Géricault   *Musée de Lyon*

14 VENUS WOUNDED BY DIOMEDES

J. D. Ingres   *Baron R. von Hirsch*

15   TASSO IN PRISON

E. Delacroix   *Kenneth Clark, Esq.*

III

THE ESCAPE IN TIME AND SPACE

THERE is no need to explain to the present generation that a great European war is inevitably followed by a period of profound discouragement. The collapse of old institutions and the emergence of new ideals can be an exciting and heartening process, as Wordsworth found it at the beginning of the French Revolution; but at the end of the conflict, when the old institutions have crashed and the new ideals have not been accomplished, there arises a general feeling of disillusionment which issues on the one hand in a cynical search for pleasure and on the other in an attempt to escape from a world from which, unlike Pandora's box, even hope has departed. Much has been made of the fact that those who were growing up to manhood in the eighteen-twenties had been conceived in intolerable stress and excitement, but this is not the whole story, for Frenchmen of that period had suffered one or other of two terrible disappointments, and some had suffered both. The French Revolution had not inaugurated the millennium, and the Restoration had not restored the ancient glories of the French monarchy. David's unrealized dream of the perfect Republican State has been dealt with in the last chapter. The majority of Frenchmen under Louis XVIII followed the Bourbons at least in this, that they looked back to the earlier days of the French monarchy, and constructed an imaginary medieval paradise into which they could escape from the pressure of the present.

Medievalism indeed was in the air of all Europe, and the French had only been protected from it by the wars of Napoleon. They were not long in discovering Sir Walter Scott, and within their own borders they felt the influence of Chateaubriand, and of his attempt to restore a somewhat theatricalized Christianity. The stained-glass windows which the Revolution had broken were now restored, at least in fancy. The monks which the

D

Jacobins had slaughtered or expelled became figures of romantic legend. The medieval castles which the men of 1794 had tried to destroy arose again as refuges for the imagination. Costume itself began to ape the modes of the Valois and of all earlier epochs—one hotchpotch of historical inaccuracy. The very chairs on which men sat began to grow Gothic.

We have already mentioned Ingres' concession to the 'Style Troubadour,' but he was only one among many. The historical genre was soon a commonplace of public exhibitions. This was the escape in time, the flight into other epochs, which is one of the most permanent impulses of the human mind, and lies at the back of all the fancies about the good old days, from the Golden Age to the Garden of Eden.

But there is another escape possible from the realities of the present: the escape in space. Not only was there a distant time when the affairs of the world were better ordered than today; there is a far country, and the nostalgia for this far country infected the greater part of young people and many older ones in the years following the Napoleonic wars; and, as so often happens, the focus of the day-dream was the Near East.

The Levant, Turkey and the Mohammedan countries generally have always exercised a powerful influence on the imaginations of Western men, and, it must be confessed, of many Western women too. There are moments when every man fancies himself a Pasha, and there are moments too when almost every woman tires of the comparative freedom she has obtained and longs to be dominated as the woman of the harem is dominated by her lord. An interesting study could be made of the psychological problems involved in this recurring dream which was never more prevalent than during the early years of the Romantic Period.

Its revival had been due in part to Napoleon himself. The ormolu sphinxes' heads on Empire furniture were due to his Egyptian campaign, but the Egypt of the Pharaohs was too remote to awaken much echo in the Western imagination. What people dreamt about was the Egypt of the Pashas, but almost indeed anywhere in the Eastern Mediterranean would do.

This influence was reinforced by the meteoric rise to fame of one man —Byron, the perfect romantic hero who seemed to sum up in his own personality all the appetites and day-dreams of the period. He was a peer (peers are still vaguely romantic to most people, even today); he had travelled in the Near East; he had expressed its conflict and its passion in widely read verse, and he had died fighting in Greece against the Turkish power. He was also something of a Turk himself in his unbridled licence and his treatment of women, and he had just the touch of *diablerie* needed to make the romantic portrait complete. Much of the painting of the Romantic Period in France remains incomprehensible unless we realize that there was an element of Byronism not only in the painters themselves but in almost everybody else.

That the mind of Delacroix had already turned to the Orient can be seen in his painting, '*Le Massacre de Scio*,' exhibited in the Salon of 1824. For the subject of '*La Mort de Sardanapale*' he went not only to a distant country but to a distant epoch; but the impulse was the same. In 1832 he eagerly seized the opportunity of going to Morocco in the suite of the French Ambassador to the Sultan, and the journey resulted in a whole group of Oriental pictures which he exhibited soon after his return to Paris. They excited the greatest admiration and the greatest hostility, but the hostility which they aroused, it is interesting to note, had little or nothing to do with their subject-matter. The most conservative public is always grateful for a novelty of subject-matter; what it will not endure is a novelty of handling, and this was obvious from the first in all Delacroix' paintings. He broke entirely with the technical methods of his contemporaries and painted in a manner which was partly his own and partly based on the practice of the Baroque.

So far from attempting to hide his brushwork, he exaggerated it. Instead of striving for a smooth surface finish he delighted in a rugosity which seems smooth enough by comparison with the strong impasto of some of the later Impressionists, but was startling in its day. His colour was purposely broken; his forms angular and violent. He painted the blood and passion of the Orient, and there must have been many, even among those who shared a similar dream, who would have preferred the calm, static odalisques of Ingres. Those who wished to treat painting merely as an escape found Delacroix' escape too rapid and too exciting. His art was no smooth chariot bearing them away with magical ease into the countries of their imagination, but the courser of Mazeppa, carrying them bound hand and foot on its back, over rocks and down precipices, through swirling streams into gloomy forests, pursued ever by the howling of innumerable wolves. The guardians of French painting did not like the work of Delacroix, and they excluded him from their official bodies until almost the end of his life.

The harshness of Delacroix is, however, nothing beside the brutality of Géricault. Théodore Géricault was older than Delacroix and died when the latter painter was scarcely at the beginning of his career. He came too early for the Oriental wave, and his early works, painted while Napoleon was still Emperor, were concerned with contemporary military subjects; but he brought to them a violence of action and a harshness of colour which distinguishes him sharply from the contemporary recorders of the Napoleonic epoch and makes him the true forerunner of the Romantic movement.

His most famous picture, 'Le Radeau de la Méduse,' was painted in 1818 and exhibited at the Salon in the following year. It owed its immense success partly to political reasons—the wreck of the *Medusa* was a recent happening and the survivors had been driven into cannibalism. The Opposition held the Government responsible and therefore welcomed Géricault's picture as admirable propaganda for their cause, but its emotional success with a larger public may be traced to the vein of horror and sadism to be found in it, and indeed in all the work of this painter. There is a larger vein of sadism in the human heart than most humanitarians are willing to admit, and if the impulse can be linked with and justified by moral and political indignation, the success of an appeal to it is assured. Géricault had considerable merit as a painter, but it is doubtful, even if he had not died at the early age of thirty-three, whether he would have successfully competed with Delacroix as the real leader of the new movement.

Both Géricault and Delacroix conform to the idea of the artist as rebel, which has become so much a part of the popular conception that it is difficult for us to realize that it was ever otherwise. Yet such a notion would have seemed extraordinary to men of a previous age, except perhaps the rebel painters of the early seventeenth century: to Caravaggio, and to Salvator Rosa, who were the real founders of the romantic tradition in painting.

24

16   THE EXECUTION OF THE DOGE MARINO FALIERO

E. Delacroix

The Wallace Collection, London

17 ST. GEORGE

E. Delacroix   *Musée de Grenoble*

18 WOMAN WITH A PARROT

E. Delacroix   *Musée de Lyon*

19   HORSES COMING OUT OF THE SEA

E. Delacroix   *Madame E. Staub-Terlinden*

20   ARABS ON THE MARCH

E. Delacroix   *Dr. H. de Rothschild*

21   PORTRAIT OF HENRI HUGUES

E. Delacroix

M. Paul Rosenberg

Raphael and Rubens never regarded themselves as rebels. A painter like Boucher must have thought of himself as half a craftsman and half a public official. It was left to the nineteenth century to establish the notion that the artist is always in rebellion against his epoch; and the fault for that belongs at least as much to the nineteenth century as to the artist. Young and unsuccessful artists—indeed the whole world of art students—seized eagerly upon the example of such men as Géricault and Delacroix to prove to themselves that their own lack of recognition was part of a general conspiracy. The artist and the bourgeois were bound to a perpetual hostility, no temporary misunderstanding, but part of the nature of things; and it must be admitted that the bourgeois of the nineteenth century showed himself much less capable of appreciating innovations in Art than the aristocratic patrons of former ages. The artist became conscious of a gulf between himself and the rest of the world which he made little attempt to cross and even did his best to widen.

The position of the art student helped to intensify and perpetuate this state of affairs. There was no temptation for the painter-apprentice of former ages to cultivate a wilful eccentricity of dress and manner. It certainly would not have helped him in his profession and it is doubtful if his master would have allowed it. But once the old system of apprenticeship had collapsed, the art student became a kind of gypsy, camping in a special quarter of a great city, and working spasmodically in the *ateliers* of well-known painters, but for the greater part of his time left to his own devices. His condition was often one of extreme poverty, as most parents strongly objected to their sons taking up so hazardous a profession as Art, and a good deal of the eccentricity of the *rapin* was due to a laudable attempt to put a good face on a bad business. The licence also of life in the *Quartier Latin* attracted many who would not otherwise have thought of being artists, and the kind of life they led has been depicted for ever—probably with very little exaggeration—in the pages of Murger's *Vie de Bohême*. It may well be doubted whether such conditions are the ideal environment for the budding of a young talent.

There is another aspect of the matter to be considered. The collapse of the old system of patronage had put painting on a level with any other

E   25

kind of manufactured goods created for a problematical demand. Such goods can only be sold, as the mercantile world was not slow in realizing, by advertisement, and paintings were no exception to this general rule. How were paintings to be advertised? Most pressing problem of all: how were the paintings of unknown young men to be advertised? How could the young artist advertise himself? He soon found that he could only advertise himself by attracting the public attention in some way, by some outrageous eccentricity which led the general public to recognize him at once as an artist, with the hope, often disappointed, that the next question would be: 'What is his name?' Even so considerable a painter as Whistler practised this kind of personal publicity throughout his long life, and with great success, by combining with a certain eccentricity of dress a dandyism of his own, which led people not only to recognize him at sight as an artist but to add almost immediately: 'That is Whistler.'

Such methods have now fallen into disuse, partly because of the lack in the modern world of a place where an artist can show himself. But the idea of the artist as an eccentrically dressed person persisted, and this relic of a romantic tradition can be seen even in the modern world, in the tendency to regard an artist as a man who deserts his wife and does not pay his bills— a gross libel on the greater part of the painting community.

Apart from its social effect, the history of romantic painting is the same as that of every other artistic impulse. That is to say, it dwindles down to a succession of imitators of imitators, until it finds its natural place in the Salon as one of the recognized modes of picture manufacture. As always, the imitators seized upon the inessential, and with a brush that knew nothing of the divine intoxication of Delacroix depicted an endless series of Oriental scenes which vied in popularity with the Salon nudes derived from Ingres and David. Delacroix' subject-matter degenerated into a welter of anecdotal exoticism, but his technical procedure represented a real innovation which was to prove one of the foundations of Impressionist practice. But the Impressionists were still in the future, and there are other currents of French painting to be considered first.

26

NOTES ON ARTISTS AND PICTURES

DELACROIX, FERDINAND-VICTOR-EUGÈNE
1798–1863

Eugène Delacroix was born at Charenton-Saint-Maurice, near Paris, in 1798. His father remained in high official positions throughout the consecutive governments of the Republic, the Directory, the Consulate and the Empire. His mother was the daughter of Oeben and the step-daughter of Riesener, both famous cabinet-makers. Delacroix was educated at the Lycée Impérial (now Louis-le-Grand), and in 1816 joined the studio of Pierre Guérin. The death of his parents in 1819 left him in great material difficulties, but he did not have to wait long for the public recognition of his talent. In 1820 he executed a painting for a convent at Nantes; at the Salon of 1822 his 'Dante et Virgile conduits par Phlégias' (Louvre) was acquired by the State, as was, in 1824, his 'Massacres de Scio' (Louvre). During the following years he received various commissions for decorations, including those of the Salles du Conseil d'État at the Louvre. In 1830 Louis-Philippe purchased his 'La Liberté guidant le Peuple' (Louvre). In 1831 he received the Legion of Honour, and the following year accompanied the Comte de Morny's mission to Morocco. Between 1833 and 1855 he was engaged on his vast decorative schemes at the Chambre des Députés, the Luxembourg, the Hôtel de Ville and the Gallerie d'Apollon in the Louvre, and also produced some of his greatest canvases, such as 'La Bataille de Taillebourg' (Rouen), 'La Justice de Trajan' (Rouen) and 'La Prise de Constantinople par les Croisés' (Louvre). At the International Exhibition of 1855 he was, like Ingres, given a gallery to himself, and in 1857 he was elected to the Institute, taking the seat of Paul Delaroche, who had died the year before. Delacroix never married, considering that the career of an artist called for 'isolation, the sacrifice of nearly all the feelings which inspire ordinary men.' A relentless worker, he had experienced great success though he had also passed through periods of great poverty. Towards the end of his life his health began to fail and he had to give up work on a large scale, but he continued to paint until his death, reviving on small canvases memories of the East which had captivated him in his youth. He died in Paris in 1863.

15. TASSO IN PRISON.

Oil on canvas, $19 \times 23\frac{3}{4}$ inches.

Inspired Baudelaire to write the following sonnet:

> Le poète au cachot, débraillé, maladif,
> Roulant un manuscrit sous son pied convulsif,
> Mesure d'un regard que la terreur enflamme
> L'escalier de vertige où s'abîme son âme.
>
> Les rires enivrants dont s'emplit la prison
> Vers l'étrange et l'absurde invitent sa raison:
> Le Doute l'environne, et la Peur ridicule,
> Hideuse et multiforme, autour de lui circule.
>
> Ce génie enfermé dans un taudis malsain,
> Ces grimaces, ces cris, ces spectres dont l'essaim
> Tourbillonne, ameuté derrière son oreille,
>
> Ce rêveur que l'horreur de son logis réveille,
> Voilà bien ton emblème, Âme aux songes obscurs
> Que le Réel étouffe entre ses quatre murs.

Painted about 1824.
First exhibited at the Salon of 1839.
Formerly the property of Alexandre Dumas, père, and Alexandre Dumas, fils.
Coll.: *Kenneth Clark, Esq., London.*

16. THE EXECUTION OF THE DOGE MARINO FALIERO.

Oil on canvas, $56\frac{7}{8} \times 44\frac{3}{8}$ inches.

This picture, which Delacroix is said to have liked best of all his works, was inspired by Byron's tragedy 'Marino Faliero.' The setting is a free rendering of the Giants' Staircase of the Palazzo Ducale, Venice. On the open book held up by the dragon on the right appears the inscription: PAX TIBI MARCE EVANGELISTA MEUS.

Signed: *Eug. Delacroix f^bat.*

Painted in 1826. First exhibited at the Paris Salon in 1827 and the following year at the British Institute, London. Originally sold by the artist for 1200 francs, then

22   THE TRUMPETER

T. Géricault   *Belvedere Museum, Vienna*

T. Géricault

23 THE MADWOMAN

Musée de Lyon

T. Géricault

24 THE MADMAN

Dr. O. Reinhart

bought back for 3000 francs. Sold again in 1856 to Bournet-Aubertot for 12,000 francs. In 1868 purchased by Lord Hertford from Isaac Pereire for £4000.

There is a sketch for this picture in the collection of Mr. Léon-Helft, fils.
Coll.: *The Wallace Collection, London.*

17. ST. GEORGE.

Oil on canvas, $18 \times 21\frac{1}{2}$ inches.

A larger replica of a picture in the Louvre, painted in 1854.

The subject has been also interpreted as 'Perseus and Andromeda' and 'Roger delivering Angelica,' but in the catalogues of both the Louvre and the Grenoble Museum it is stated to be 'St. George.'

Acquired by the Museum in 1858 from the Arosa collection.
Coll.: *Musée de Grenoble.*

18. WOMAN WITH A PARROT.

Oil on canvas, $9\frac{3}{4} \times 12\frac{1}{2}$ inches.

Signed and dated 1827.

First exhibited at the Salon of 1827.

Presented to the Museum by M. Couturier de Royas in 1897.
Coll.: *Musée de Lyon.*

19. HORSES COMING OUT OF THE SEA.

Oil on canvas, 20×24 inches.

Signed and dated 1860.

Former collections: Marquis de Lau; Edwards; Fanien; Faure; Laurent-Richard; Mame; Esnault-Pelterie; Denys-Cochin.
Coll.: *Mme. Emil Staub-Terlinden, Männedorf, Switzerland.*

20. ARABS ON THE MARCH.

Oil on canvas, $21\frac{1}{2} \times 25\frac{1}{2}$ inches.

Signed: *Eug. Delacroix*, and dated: *1855.*

Engraved by Veyrassat.

Former collections: Michel de Trétaigne; Baronne de Rothschild.
Coll.: *Dr. Henri de Rothschild, Paris.*

21. PORTRAIT OF HENRI HUGUES.

Oil on canvas, $29\frac{1}{4} \times 24$ inches.

Henri Hugues, a post-office official and amateur-poet, was a cousin of Delacroix. Painted in 1839 and presented by the artist to Léon Riesener, another cousin.

Former collections: L. Riesener; Mme. Léouzon-le-Duc.
Coll.: *M. Paul Rosenberg, Paris.*

GÉRICAULT, JEAN-LOUIS-ANDRÉ-THÉODORE
1791–1824

Théodore Géricault was born in 1791. He was a native of Rouen, but his parents, who were wealthy *bourgeois*, moved to Paris when he was still a child. In 1808 he joined the studio of Carle Vernet, whom he left two years later to work with Guérin. But strictly classical training had little appeal for him; his admiration went out to Gros and to such old masters as Rubens, Titian, Rembrandt and Van Dyck, of whose works in the Louvre he made numerous freely treated copies. He made his *début* at the Salon in 1812 with 'Officier de Chasseurs à Cheval Chargeant' (Louvre), which brought him a gold medal. He was at that time so attracted by the beauty of uniforms that he enlisted and served some time in the army. In 1816, after an unhappy love affair, he decided to leave France and went to Florence and Rome, where he stayed until 1818. On his return to Paris he produced his best known work, 'Le Radeau de la Méduse' (Louvre), which was exhibited at the Salon of 1819. In the following year, an exhibition of this picture having been arranged in London, Géricault came to England, where he spent two years painting his various studies of horses and jockeys. He returned to Paris in 1822 and died there in 1824, after a riding accident, from an affection of the spine.

13. SLAVES HOLDING A HORSE. (*Épisode de la Course de Chevaux Libres.*)
     Oil on canvas, $18\frac{1}{8} \times 23\frac{1}{4}$ inches.
     A sketch for a painting which was never executed, inspired by the so-called race of the *Barberi* in Rome. Another version of the same subject is in the Louvre, and a sketch for it in the collection of Mme. A. Tordeux.
     Painted about 1817.
     Acquired by the Museum in 1866.
     Coll.: *Musée de Rouen.*

22. THE TRUMPETER.
     Oil on canvas, $18\frac{1}{8} \times 15$ inches.
     Painted in 1813-14.
     Purchased by the Museum in 1924 from the Sarlin collection.
     Coll.: *Belvedere Museum, Vienna.*

E. Isabey

25   A PROMENADE BY THE SEA

The Wallace Collection, London

26   ESTHER ADORNING HERSELF TO APPEAR BEFORE AHAZUERUS

T. Chassériau   Baron A. Chassériau

27 THE APPARITION

G. Moreau

Musée du Louvre, Paris

28　THE PRODIGAL SON

P. Puvis de Chavannes

M. G. Lerolle

23. THE MADWOMAN. (*La Folle.*)

Oil on canvas, $25\frac{1}{2} \times 21\frac{1}{4}$ inches.

Sometimes referred to as 'La Hyène de la Salpêtrière.'

This and the picture on fig. 24 belong to a series of studies which Géricault executed between 1821 and 1824 for Dr. Georget, chief doctor at the Salpêtrière. The pictures represent inmates of the hospital, the woman here portrayed being afflicted by the mania of envy. Other paintings of the same series are in the collection of the Duc de Trévise, Paris, and in the Ghent Museum.

Former collections: the painter Charles Jacque; Chéramy, Paris (acquired by the Museum at his sale in 1908).

Coll.: *Musée de Lyon.*

24. THE MADMAN.

Oil on canvas, $31\frac{3}{4} \times 25\frac{1}{2}$ inches.

See previous notice.

Coll.: *Dr. Oskar Reinhart, Winterthur, Switzerland.*

ISABEY, LOUIS-GABRIEL-EUGÈNE

1804–1886

Isabey was born in Paris in 1804; Jean-Baptiste Isabey, the famous miniature painter, was his father and master. But he soon forsook the classical tradition in which he was brought up and became an enthusiastic follower of the Romantic movement. He made his first appearance at the Salon of 1824 when he exhibited marine subjects and landscapes. In 1830 he accompanied the French navy on its expedition to Algiers as official draughtsman.

Of a charming and benevolent disposition, Isabey was very popular with his contemporaries as a man as well as a painter. Society and artists frequently assembled in his *hôtel* in the Avenue Frochot, and he seldom refused to help those in distress. He died in Paris in 1886.

25. A PROMENADE BY THE SEA.

Oil on canvas, $19\frac{1}{4} \times 26\frac{1}{4}$ inches.

Signed: *E. Isabey*, and dated: *46*.

Coll.: *The Wallace Collection, London.*

31

CHASSÉRIAU, THÉODORE
1819–1856

Chassériau was born in 1819 at Sainte-Barbe de Samana in the Antilles of French parents. He came to Paris when a child and entered the École des Beaux-Arts in 1833 as a pupil of Ingres, whom he later followed to Rome. Subsequently he conceived a great admiration of Delacroix and gave up Classicism for Romanticism. He first exhibited at the Salon in 1836. He did mural decorations in several Paris churches and at the Palais d'Orsay. His death occurred in Paris in 1856.

26. ESTHER ADORNING HERSELF TO APPEAR BEFORE AHAZUERUS.
> Oil on canvas, $17\frac{3}{4} \times 14\frac{1}{2}$ inches.
> Painted in 1841 and first exhibited at the Salon in the following year.
> Signed: *Th^{re} Chassériau*, and dated: *1841*.
> Coll.: *Baron Arthur Chassériau, Paris*.

MOREAU, GUSTAVE
1826–1897

Gustave Moreau, who was born in Paris in 1826, was the son of an architect. In 1846 he joined the class of Picot at the École des Beaux-Arts, and seven years later made his first appearance at the Salon, where he exhibited a '*Pietà*' (Frankfurt). He was made a member of the Institute in 1888, and in 1891 succeeded Elie Delaunay as professor at the École des Beaux-Arts. Henri Matisse, Albert Marquet and Georges Rouault were among his pupils. On his death, which occurred in Paris in 1897, he bequeathed to the State his house (now the *Musée Gustave Moreau*) with all the paintings, drawings and engravings which it contained.

Moreau's exotic mysticism, and the literary trend of his paintings, had a great appeal for certain contemporary authors. Lengthy descriptions of his pictures are given by J-K. Huysmans in *À Rebours* and by Jean Lorrain in *Monsieur de Phocas*.

27. THE APPARITION.
> Oil on canvas, $41\frac{3}{8} \times 28\frac{1}{4}$ inches.
> Coll.: *Musée du Louvre, Paris*.

PUVIS DE CHAVANNES, PIERRE-CÉCIL
1824–1898

Puvis de Chavannes was born at Lyons in 1824 of a family which traced its ancestry back to 1152. He went to Paris in 1844 and studied for short periods with Henry Scheffer, Delacroix and Couture. When he was thirty he met the Princess Maria Cantacuzène, who became his lifelong friend but whom he did not marry until 1897. She was the model for 'Sainte Geneviève watching over Paris,' the mural painting in the Panthéon which Puvis executed in 1898—the year when both he and his wife died within an interval of two months. Puvis is best known for the extensive mural compositions which he painted for the Hôtel de Ville, the Sorbonne and the Panthéon in Paris.

28. THE PRODIGAL SON.
    Oil on panel, $50\frac{3}{8} \times 37\frac{3}{8}$ inches.
    Signed and dated 1879.
    Coll.: *M. Guillaume Lerolle, Paris.*

FANTIN-LATOUR, IGNACE-HENRI-JEAN-THÉODORE
1836–1904

Henri Fantin-Latour was born at Grenoble in 1836. His father was a French painter of Italian descent, and his mother a Russian. He received his first artistic tuition from his father, and later joined the class of a certain Lecoq-de-Boisbaudran in Paris. He also studied for a short while at the École des Beaux-Arts. In 1861 he made his *début* at the Salon where, except in 1868, 1880 and 1882, he exhibited yearly from 1864 to 1899. He was also a regular exhibitor at the Royal Academy and the Institute of Painters in Oil. He paid several visits to London, where he had two great friends in Whistler and Edwin Edwards, the lawyer-artist. He died suddenly at his country house at Buré (Orne) in 1904.

29. 'LA FÉERIE.'
    Oil on canvas, $38\frac{5}{8} \times 51\frac{1}{4}$ inches.

G

33

When Fantin-Latour sent this picture to the Salon of 1863 it was rejected by the jury. It was exhibited the same year at the Salon des Refusés and lent in 1864 to Whistler, who kept it in London until 1889, when it was returned to the artist and sold by him to Édouard Haviland.

Signed and dated 1863.

Former collections: Ed. Haviland, Paris; Private collection, Scotland; Lefèvre Galleries, London.

Coll.: *Art Association, Montreal, Canada.*

97. STILL LIFE.

Oil on canvas, $12\frac{1}{2} \times 11\frac{1}{2}$ inches.

This picture is sometimes known as '*Nature Morte de Fiançailles,*' as it was presented by the artist to Mlle. Victoire Dubourg as a wedding gift.

Signed: *Fantin*, dated: *1896*.

Coll.: *Musée de Grenoble.*

H. Fantin-Latour

29 "LA FÉERIE"

J. B. C. Corot

30   HONFLEUR: HOUSES   ON   THE   QUAY

Madame E. Staub-Terlinden

IV

THE ESCAPE FROM THE TOWN

THE countryman is never sentimental about the country, and there is no passionate love of landscape until the tone of life is predominantly urban. This is not to say that the countryman does not appreciate the beauties around him; his open-air life may give him a feeling of well-being, especially if the day is fine. The sight of a growing field of wheat may provoke emotions which are at least partly aesthetic; but Nature is too much a part of his everyday life to be the substance of which his dreams are made. In primitive times no one escapes to the country unless he is a bandit. If he is an honest man he escapes from marauders to the protection of the neighbouring town, and even in more settled times people rarely admire the countryside unless it is 'smiling' or 'verdurous.' Mountains are obstacles; they are 'horrid' rather than majestic; wild moors are so much waste land; woods are things to be cleared away; swirling rivers things to be tamed, bridged or merely avoided. This is the universal attitude in early times, that is pre-industrial times, and it persisted even among town dwellers until well on into the eighteenth century.

Painting in this, as in so much else, faithfully reflects the dominant tone of men's thoughts. Landscape (with certain seventeenth-century exceptions which are themselves the precursors of romantic painting) is thought of as a background for figures, even if those figures are sentimentalized country people. Exquisite little landscapes are to be found in the background of Renaissance portraits or sacred subject-pictures, but they were not thought sufficient in themselves to justify making a picture of them. It is no accident that the Dutch, who were the first to evolve the urban mercantile life which in the nineteenth century became the life of almost everybody, were also the first to paint landscape for its own sake.

35

The late eighteenth century witnessed a widespread revolt against highly organized life in general and city life in particular. Even Marie Antoinette played at being a milkmaid, and the followers of Rousseau made no secret of their opinion that, in theory at least, the rural life was the only tolerable one. How little the realities of rural life were understood may be judged from the sentimental peasant pictures so numerous in France towards the end of the eighteenth century, pictures in which all shepherdesses were pretty and all milkmaids daintily attired. This does not, however, affect the fact that there was a growing tendency to regard the town as enervating and corrupt and to look upon the country as a spiritual refuge. Wordsworth was a man who had the strength of mind to carry his ideals into practice, but he was not the only hermit of his period, still less was he the only one in whom the impulse could have been found.

The love of the country for its own sake seems to have arisen earlier in England than in France, and by the end of the eighteenth century the early English landscapists record some of their greatest triumphs both in oil and water colour. Now, the most striking thing about the men of the French Revolution, apart from their enthusiasm for the Ancient World, was their anglomania. For a short time everything English was admired. English institutions, English habits of life, even English clothes, and it is one of the curiosities of the history of costume that the men of 1789, while they thought of themselves as Ancient Romans, clothed themselves as English country gentlemen.

Enthusiasm for things English was naturally obscured by the Napoleonic wars, but it was not obliterated, and after Waterloo English influences flowed into France once more. France by this time had become conscious too of an Industrial Revolution, and although industrial towns in France rarely equalled the ugliness of their English counterparts, they gave an added impulse to the flight into the country, characteristic of an industrial age. So long as French painting was occupied with classical reconstructions, or neo-medieval *genre* pieces, or with the Orientalism of the early romantic manner, the influences we have been discussing had naturally but little scope; but when French painters turned to the country and tried to elaborate a school of pure landscape painting, they turned to the English for inspiration, and beyond them to the Dutch painters, on whose work the English tradition was itself founded. We have grown nowadays so accustomed to take the lead from Paris that it is hard to believe that at the beginning of the nineteenth century the French looked on the English as their masters.

Delacroix himself, who was in England in the eighteen-twenties, confessed himself as having been influenced by Constable. The debt of lesser men is even more obvious, both to Constable and to the short-lived English master, Richard Parkes Bonington. But not all French painters could come to England, English paintings were rarely exhibited in Paris, and the day of good reproductions was still in the future. So while much of their impulse came from England, many of the French landscapists of the period we are discussing went to the seventeenth-century Dutchmen for their direct inspiration. Rousseau founded himself upon the Ruysdael, and as Rousseau is the central figure, although by no means the greatest painter, of the so-called Barbizon School, many of the productions of that school have a distinctly Dutch look. Ruysdael, however, did not paint the Dutch countryside around him, but preferred to paint imaginary scenes of a mountainous region he had never visited, and some of this faint air of theatricality is carried over into the early paintings of the Barbizon School, in spite of their quite Ruskinian devotion to the details of the scene which lay before them.

It is the fashion nowadays to depreciate their products because they did not construct their landscapes on the architectural principles worked out by Cézanne half a century later. They are none the less of considerable importance if only because, as Mr. Clive Bell so happily expresses it, 'They made of Constable's splendid but idiosyncratic and untidy vernacular a teachable language of widest application, in which competent students of any nationality might learn, as only too many have learned, to paint what they have been taught to observe. This was of importance because the new instrument for recording observations fell into the hands of the Impressionists, who were beholden to it as a poet of genius might be beholden to some unusually sensible grammar unearthed from a dusty corner in a schoolmaster's library.' Even this is an understatement; for it is not to underestimate the importance of Cézanne to say that there are other kinds of landscape painting than the rigidly constructional kind that the genius of the late nineteenth-century master seems for the moment to have imposed for ever.

The term 'Barbizon School' is, like most such terms, largely a misnomer, seeing that by no means all the painters who are supposed to have belonged to it painted in the Forest of Fontainebleau, but it is a useful label for a kind of attitude towards Art which was shared by Rousseau, Daubigny, Harpignies and to some extent by Charles Jacque and Troyon. With them is usually associated Corot, a painter who is paying now for his extraordinary popularity in the second half of the nineteenth century. Modern critics may admire the landscape of his first Roman Period, or the paintings which he produced between 1822 and 1825 at Rouen and on the Normandy coast, but they will have nothing to do with the somewhat grey and fluffy landscapes of his later years, although these were undoubtedly the paintings which the general public admired. Mr. Wilenski, whose services to the study of French painting needs no stressing, even goes so far as to say that Corot's later landscapes were founded upon photographs, and that the famous fluffy effect was due to the painter's deliberate imitation of foliage slightly out of focus. But if his characteristic treatment of trees begins, as is generally agreed, about 1848, it would be interesting to know how many photographs of *landscapes* were in existence at that period. There cannot have been very many of them; and it is at least arguable that, if modern photographs of landscapes tend to be blurred in outline, this is due to an attempt to imitate the effect of painting, particularly the paintings of Corot.

Corot had a strong streak of poetry in his nature, of that literary poetry, if you will, which is anathema to the modern aesthetic puritans. He came to prefer a certain moment of twilight when the foliage *is* blurred, when the outlines of trees lose their architectural qualities and become merely deeper shadows in the evening mists. He liked painting that sort of thing, which in itself is surely no crime; but unfortunately the public liked it too, liked it only too well, and Corot was led almost insensibly to repeat his effects and to allow his manner to degenerate into a mannerism. The disgust of the critics is intensified by the fact that it was this mannerism

J. B. C. Corot

31   ROME: THE FORUM FROM THE FARNESE GARDENS

Baron Gou-gaud

32 ITALIAN WOMAN PLAYING THE MANDOLINE

J. B. C. Corot

Dr. O. Reinhart

that the public admired, and this admiration unfortunately gave rise to a number of pseudo-Corots even greater than the very considerable *œuvre* of the master himself.

The figures introduced into Corot's paintings have no great significance, and the majority of the painters above mentioned, with the obvious exception of Jacque, were interested chiefly in pure landscape, in the countryside, not in its inhabitants. But it was inevitable that painting should be influenced by the humanitarian enthusiasm so characteristic of the middle of the nineteenth century, and a new school of peasant painters arose, less fanciful and artificial than those of the reign of Louis XVI, but even more idealized and sentimental. The greatest of these was Millet, who has suffered badly in recent years from the reaction against sentiment of any kind in Art, and particularly in painting.

Millet, no doubt, thought he was being extremely realistic when he refrained from adding ribbons to the dresses of his shepherdesses in the eighteenth-century manner. But naturalism was hardly his intention; he was Wordsworth rather than Crabbe. He deliberately shut his eyes to all the disagreeable, and seemingly inevitable, strains of peasant character— its avarice, its day-to-day pettiness—and chose to depict the peasant as the only true hero, a man perpetually at odds with Nature, not in any glorious and spectacular fashion, but none the less noble in his unshakable persistence, wringing from the soil the bare minimum of a livelihood.

If any man ever had the right to depict the heroism of the life of poverty it was certainly Millet himself. From the time when he settled at Barbizon in 1849 his life was one perpetual struggle, and on one occasion the payment for a picture arrived only just in time, for the Millet family had eaten nothing for two days. For the 'Angelus,' a picture which has probably been more widely distributed in reproductions than any other work ever painted, he received forty pounds, and to the end of his life he remained 'the simple cottager' he had always been, and it is probable that he desired nothing better.

It is easy with Mr. Clive Bell to call Millet a prig, but even that severe critic is constrained to admit that he was a greatly gifted prig and that there is no escaping a man so conscious of his honourable independence and ambition in life. We may agree, however, that his larger pictures, even apart from the sentiment which the modern world finds it so difficult to forgive, are rarely completely satisfactory. He simplified the drawing of his figures in order to give them a greater monumental weight and dignity, yet that simplification sometimes seems summary, arbitrary and a little empty. His colour is rarely satisfactory, for colour must either be used in the modern architectural way as part of the structure of recession, or it must be used for its own sensuous qualities. Of the former of these two possibilities Millet knew nothing; to the latter he was completely indifferent. And perhaps he strove, consciously or half consciously, to make his colour harsh and unpleasing as if to emphasize the privations and hardships of the life he chose to depict.

Of course, Millet's sentiment found a host of imitators, and the boneless ineptitude of their works does something to excuse the severity with which Millet himself is judged. The whole history of Art is the history of such progressive degeneration, and it is unfair to judge any master by the disciples who seize upon the inessentials of his work. The studies of his drawings at any rate should convince any unprejudiced observer that Millet was a very respectable artist, even if the movement which he originated ended in a morass.

COROT, JEAN-BAPTISTE-CAMILLE
1796–1875

Corot, who was born in Paris in 1796, was the son of a hairdresser and a milliner. In his youth he worked in a drapery business, spending all his spare time drawing and painting. At first his parents looked askance at his desire to become a painter, but a small allowance which his father settled upon him when he was twenty-six years old enabled him to give up his job and devote himself entirely to art. He then spent most of his time in the country north of Paris, painting landscapes from nature. In 1825 he went to Italy, where he stayed for three years. On his return he painted mostly at Ville d'Avray and Fontainebleau. He exhibited regularly at the Salons but remained unnoticed until 1838, when the Duc d'Orléans bought two of his pictures. Soon afterwards two more were purchased by the State, and in 1846 he was decorated with the Legion of Honour. From then on his success was established. He became a rich man, but having simple tastes he continued to lead a simple and quiet life. He died in Paris in 1875, mourned by the numerous people whose needs, in his great generosity of heart, he had helped to relieve.

30. HONFLEUR: HOUSES ON THE QUAY.
>   Oil on canvas, $15\frac{1}{4} \times 21\frac{3}{4}$ inches.
> Painted about 1830.
> Signed.
> Former collections: Corot Sale, 1875; Lefèbvre, Roubaix (sold at the Lefèbvre sale in 1896 for 4700 francs); Dr. Dieulafoy, Paris; Marquis de Rochegouste, Paris.
>   Coll.: *Mme. Emil Staub-Terlinden, Männedorf, Switzerland.*

31. ROME: THE FORUM FROM THE FARNESE GARDENS.
>   Oil on canvas, $18\frac{1}{2} \times 32$ inches.

H

During his stay in Rome in 1826 Corot did a painting of the Forum, now in the Louvre, from which the present picture was painted in 1845 for M. Robert of Mantes. The trees in the foreground do not exist in the original study.

Signed: *Corot*, and dated: *1845*.

Coll.: *Baron Napoléon Gourgaud, Paris*.

32. ITALIAN WOMAN PLAYING THE MANDOLINE.

Oil on canvas, $23\frac{7}{8} \times 21\frac{1}{2}$ inches.

Painted between 1865 and 1870.

Signed.

Former collections: Arosa; Brame.

Coll.: *Dr. Oskar Reinhart, Winterthur, Switzerland*.

33. WOMAN WITH A MANDOLINE.

Oil on canvas, $21\frac{1}{2} \times 15\frac{1}{4}$ inches.

Painted between 1860 and 1870.

Signed.

Coll.: *Dr. Oskar Reinhart, Winterthur, Switzerland*.

34. MOTHER AND CHILD.

Oil on canvas, $17\frac{1}{2} \times 14\frac{1}{4}$ inches.

Painted between 1860 and 1865.

Signed. There exists another variation of the same subject.

Former collections: Corot Sale, 1875; Bascle; Henri Vever; Knoedler.

Coll.: *Baron Robert von Hirsch, Basle*.

35. THE BRIDGE AT MANTES.

Oil on canvas, $18 \times 23\frac{3}{4}$ inches.

Corot visited Mantes on several occasions and painted various views of the bridge. This picture appears to have been executed between 1868 and 1870.

Signed.

Former collections: M. C. D. Borden, New York; Agnew.

Now on loan at the National Gallery, London.

Coll.: *C. S. Gulbenkian, Esq., Paris*.

36. THE CHESTNUT TREES OF MONT USSY.

Oil on canvas, $19\frac{1}{2} \times 23\frac{1}{2}$ inches.

Painted at Fontainebleau in September 1873. Sold by the artist to M. Mayer.

Signed.

Coll.: *The Tooth Galleries, London*.

37. THE ARRAS ROAD.

Oil on canvas, 24×32 inches.

J. B. C. Corot   33   WOMAN WITH A MANDOLINE   *Dr. O. Reinhart*

34   MOTHER AND CHILD   J. B. C. Corot   *Baron 2. von Hirsch*

35 THE BRIDGE AT MANTES

J. B. C. Corot   *C. S. Gulbenkian, Esq.*

36 THE CHESTNUT TREES OF MONT USSY

J. B. C. Corot   *The Tooth Galleries, London*

37 THE ARRAS ROAD

J. B. C. Corot   *Musée du Louvre, Paris*

38 A VILLAGE BY THE SEA

J. B. C. Corot   *Baron Gourgaud*

C. F. Daubigny

39 SPRING

Musée du Louvre, Paris

T. Rousseau

40 WOODLAND SCENE

Baron L. von Koenig

Though known as 'La Route d'Arras,' the picture actually represents the road of Sin-le-Noble near Douai, where Corot spent six days during July 1873. Painted from Nature, it was finished by the artist in his studio in Paris. There exists a photograph of the painting before the large branch in the left foreground was added.

Signed.

Former collections: Felix Robaut; Alfred Robaut; Tomy Thiéry.

Coll.: *Musée du Louvre, Paris.*

38. A Village by the Sea.

Oil on canvas, 18×22 inches.

Sometimes referred to as 'Le Cavalier.' Painted between 1870 and 1872.

Signed.

Former collections: Sale H. P., Paris, 1901; Arnold and Tripp; Dr. Dieulafoy, Paris.

Coll.: *Baron Napoléon Gourgaud, Paris.*

DAUBIGNY, CHARLES-FRANÇOIS
1817–1878

Charles Daubigny was born in Paris in 1817. He was the son of the landscape painter Edmé-François Daubigny, who gave him his first lessons in painting. When his mother died and his father remarried he left the paternal home, and, after a short trip to Italy, made his own living by restoring pictures for the Louvre. In 1838 he joined Paul Delaroche's class at the École de Beaux-Arts, and in the same year exhibited a 'View of Notre-Dame' at the Salon. He was awarded medals at the Salons of 1848 and 1853 as well as at the International exhibitions of 1855 and 1867. In 1857 he was entrusted with the mural decoration of the Ministry of State in the Louvre. During the last thirty years of his life he mostly led a strolling existence on the Seine and the Oise, living in a house-boat which he used as a home and a studio. Though Daubigny was on very friendly terms with the Barbizon painters and is considered as one of the group, he never actually lived at Barbizon. He died in Paris in 1878.

39. Spring.

Oil on canvas, $37\frac{3}{8} \times 75\frac{1}{2}$ inches.

Signed: *Daubigny,* and dated: *1857.*

Coll.: *Musée du Louvre, Paris.*

43

ROUSSEAU, ÉTIENNE-PIERRE-THÉODORE
1812–1867

Théodore Rousseau was born in Paris in 1812. He was the son of a tailor, who soon became aware of his son's gifts and sent him to study first under J-C-J. Rémond and then under G-G. Lethière. But academic training did not suit Rousseau and he soon left the studios to work in the open air and paint landscapes direct from nature. He had his first picture accepted at the Salon when he was only nineteen years of age. This early success was followed by a long period during which all the works he submitted were systematically refused. Not until 1848 was he again admitted to the Salon. That same year he was also commissioned by the State to paint 'La Sortie de la Forêt de Fontainebleau,' for which he received 4000 francs. From then on his reputation was established. The wooded scenes in which he specialized were much sought after and well paid for. Rousseau was always a man of simple habits and was fond of solitude. His successes did not change him; the last part of his life he spent at Barbizon, where Millet became his great friend and where he died in 1867. He is one of the foremost representatives of the school of painting which takes its name from the little village in the heart of the Fontainebleau Forest.

40. WOODLAND SCENE.
    Oil on Canvas, 37×52⅜ inches.
    Formerly in the collection of Hugo von Tschudi, Berlin.
    Coll.: *Baron Leo von Koenig, Berlin.*

BOUDIN, EUGÈNE-LOUIS
1824–1898

Boudin was born at Honfleur in 1824. At the age of twenty he opened a paper and colour shop at Le Havre, but five years later gave up commerce and decided to devote himself to art. He went to Paris, where he became the pupil of Isabey and where he married. He first exhibited at the Salon in

1859 with a picture entitled 'Le Pardon de Sainte-Anne, Palud,' which received high praise from Baudelaire. From then on he was a continual exhibitor at the Salon and also held one-man shows at Antwerp, Bordeaux and Dortrecht. If, during his lifetime, his paintings did not obtain the high prices they now fetch, he nevertheless always made a comfortable income out of the harbour and beach scenes in which he specialized. Boudin died in Paris in 1898.

41. BORDEAUX.
 Oil on canvas, $29\frac{1}{2} \times 39\frac{1}{2}$ inches.
Painted about 1870.
Signed.
Coll.: *The Tooth Galleries, London.*

42. BEACH SCENE.
 Oil on canvas, $13\frac{5}{8} \times 22\frac{1}{2}$ inches.
Signed: *E. Boudin*, and dated: *69.*
Coll.: *Elwood B. Hosmer, Esq., Canada.*

JONGKIND, JOHANN-BARTHOLD
1819–1891

Jongkind was born at Latrop, near Rotterdam, in 1819. Though a native of Holland, he spent most of his life in France, where he exerted considerable influence on the development of Impressionism and was acclaimed by Monet as '*le grand peintre.*' His work constitutes a link between the Impressionists and the Barbizon painters.

Jongkind was originally a pupil of Schelfhout at The Hague, where he struggled with extreme poverty. The grant of a pension by the King of Holland enabled him in 1846 to go to Paris, where he studied under Isabey. After returning to Holland, he finally settled in France in 1860 and lived from 1878 onward at Côte-St.-André, near Grenoble, paying occasional visits to the South and to Switzerland. His lifelong addiction to excessive eating and drinking gradually undermined his health and eventually affected

I

his reason. In 1891 he had to be taken to the Asylum of Saint-Rambert-Saint-Egrève, where he died shortly after admission.

43. ENTRANCE TO A HARBOUR.
Oil on canvas, $22\frac{3}{4} \times 31\frac{3}{4}$ inches.
Signed and dated 1865.
Formerly in the Dauber collection.
Coll.: *Lord Ivor Spencer-Churchill, London.*

E. Boudin

41 BORDEAUX

42   BEACH SCENE

E. Boudin   *Elwood B. Hosmer, Esq.*

43   ENTRANCE TO A HARBOUR

J. B. Jongkind   *Lord Ivor Spencer-Churchill*

44　THE CONCERT

A. Renoir   *M. Claude Renoir*

V

REALISM

WE have considered in the last two chapters various aspects of Art as an escape; for Humanitarianism is no less an escape than Romanticism. The School we are now to consider prided itself on not wishing to escape from anything, on accepting life in its totality, and depicting it with a maximum of fact and minimum of comment. Realism would have nothing to do either with romanticized Orientals or idealized peasants.

The Realist movement was, of course, not confined to painting. It was even more manifest in the world of letters, partly as a reaction against the extravagances of Romanticism and partly as a kind of political move-ment—a Liberal and indeed a Socialistic protest against the unrealities of public life and the extravagance of the governing classes. Its literary technique was an attempt to use the scientific method of documentation and the accumulation of evidence. It no longer attempted to tell a story in the old sense, indeed it tried to reduce subject to a minimum, and if it depicted individual passion it did so against the background of society and with a sociological intention. For the swollen egotism of the romantic writer it tried to substitute the detachment and self-effacement of the *savant*. Painting by its very nature could only display these tendencies in a very minor degree, but they were present none the less, and Courbet at least, the principal painter of the Realist School, was very conscious of his social mission. Realism was to be a clearing the mind of cant and a sweeping away of privilege.

Realism, however, is always a delusion both in painting and in literature, and although in theory the novels of Zola were supposed to be so many Blue Books, so many slices of 'life,' they were actually constructed with extreme care and were as deliberately arranged, beneath their apparently haphazard accumulation of detail, as the works of any other novelist. The

47

first chapter of *Nana* is as neat and well ordered as the opening scene of a play. The production of a work of art must always imply selection and arrangement, and the work of the best of the Realists, by which alone the movement should be judged, is no exception. Actually, Courbet, the Realist, was far less realistic in painting than many of those who were to come after him and to paint under a different label. If Realism is the absence of *parti pris* and the self-effacement of the artist, then Courbet was not a Realist at all.

None the less, he had a virile delight in the world as he found it, which, incompatible as it might be with his Socialistic principles, definitely introduced a new note into painting. His peasants are not the idealized peasants of Millet, and his '*Demoiselles de la Seine*' are just a couple of French street women out for the day, but only half on holiday. Courbet let his pictures speak for themselves, and what they said was never 'This is what ought not to be,' but simply 'This is what is.' He took no pains to make his *Baigneuses* conform to the smooth, meaningless grace of the degenerate Ingres tradition, and in consequence there seemed to Courbet's contemporaries to be a certain brutality in all his work, a harshness of vision and an insolence of presentation and handling. It was plain that the man was a vulgar fellow, if not a dangerous revolutionary, and the latter notion was the one which the artist himself made no attempt to dispel. Consciously, or half consciously, he encouraged it, and although it was to cost him dear in comfort and monetary success, it contributed also to his immense notoriety and his power as *chef d'école*. *Chef d'école* he certainly was, for the early Impressionist movement is nothing but a continuation of the Courbet tradition, and if, at the end of the nineteenth century, the triumph of the Impressionists somewhat obscured his achievements, he has now emerged once more as one of the most individual and important painters of the nineteenth century.

Courbet is the precursor but not the founder of Impressionism. When we look back upon the movement it is seen to have contained so many diverse strands, to have submitted to so many influences and to have resulted in such different kinds of painting that it is difficult to say who the founder was. In the early 'sixties the name 'Impressionist' had not been invented, but the general public was well aware that a new school had come into being, and it was unanimous in thinking that the leader of the new school was Manet. He studied, oddly enough, under Couture, but the whole course of his life was one perpetual revolt against the teaching of his master. Like every other independent spirit of the time, he was deeply influenced by Courbet, and his ideas were originally very similar. That is to say, he disliked equally the wrecks of Romanticism and the idealizing tradition of the *École de Rome*. But, unlike Courbet, he was essentially a townsman, and his early '*Buveur d'Absinthe*'—studio arrangement as it is —showed clearly his willingness to accept the life around him as the subject-matter for painting.

He early came under the influence of the Spaniards, especially of Goya, and for a time his admiration for this master diverted his eyes from contemporary life in Paris, so that he produced a series of pictures of Spanish scenes, bull-fighters and the rest, studied from studio models in costume.

These pictures were the first by which the critics became acquainted with the work of Manet, and when they were exhibited in the early part of 1862 they were greeted with a torrent of almost universal abuse, difficult to understand in retrospect unless we realize at how many points Manet was attacking the Academic tradition of his day. The critics were compelled to accept Goya as a great painter, although they did not like him. Manet seemed to them to have all the brutality and Realism of Goya with a new crudity of colour added, but it was his lack of Idealism that troubled them most, his refusal to generalize and also his refusal to paint a 'subject' as subject was then understood.

By the hostility which he aroused he had already, before the age of thirty, become the leader of a new school of painting, and as, unlike Courbet, he did not allow his energies to be diverted into political revolt, he seemed to the Academicians all the more dangerous. It was not that he was unsusceptible to ideas; on the contrary, he soon made friends with Zola and Goncourt and no doubt regarded himself as part of the general movement which they had inaugurated. By their theory of documentation and the scientific approach these writers foreshadowed one of the main later developments of Impressionism. By their insistence on the duty of the artist to

49

depict everyday life without Idealism and, in theory at least, without moral comment, they embodied another principle of Impressionism and one which was for the moment all powerful. Most people, especially those who were interested in painting, had become so used to a 'prettifying' of life, a deliberate 'ennobling' of the material which the world offered to the painter, that they were shocked almost out of their senses by Manet's 'Olympia.'

The outcry was more vehement than ever. It was permissible to paint a nude courtesan who pretended that she was Venus or a harem beauty. It was even permissible to give her some of the accessories of a past Age to remind people that the great Venetians had once treated similar subjects. But to paint her as a modern Parisienne, not particularly attractive, and with no appeal either to sentiment or eroticism, this was to go beyond the limits allowed to painting. In the opinion of many of his contemporaries the painter of such a subject was a deliberate pornographer. The indignation of the critics was even directed against Manet's technical methods, his manner of painting in broad touches with strong juxtaposition of light and shadow, his flattening of planes, his emphasis on contour, his contempt for what the Academies meant by 'linear beauty.' In short, by all the technical proceedings which were to become the commonplaces of subsequent painters.

From the later history of Impressionism Manet remained somewhat apart. He was never a *pleinairiste*, but although his later paintings show less reliance upon formal composition, they lack the apparently spontaneous and wilfully accidental *mise en toile* of other painters of the same school. In the second phase of the Impressionist movement it became the ideal of the artist to reduce his own vision to the impersonality of a camera's eye. But this development must be left to the next chapter, for it is part of the general belief in the infallibility of science which characterized the last quarter of the nineteenth century.

Manet himself was less influenced by the optical discoveries of the period than by the Japanese. Oriental art, as something quaint and amusing, had been known to the Western world for a century and a half. Chinese wallpapers had adorned the walls of mid-eighteenth-century mansions, and

45   THE SLEEPING BATHER

G. Courbet   *M. Paul Rosenberg*

46 THE PICTURE STALL

H. Daumier

Madame E. Staub-Terlinden

the rococo decorators had even evolved a *chinoiserie* of their own, but the discovery of the Japanese colour print in the late 'fifties was something quite different. For the first time Europeans began to look upon Oriental art not as something amusingly exotic, but as something deserving of imitation for the solidity of its design and the expressiveness of its contours. Whistler, who was in Paris at the time of the discovery of the Japanese print, had the whole course of his painting diverted by it, and its influence on purely French painting was no less remarkable.

Manet's elimination of *chiaroscuro* and his principle of modelling by expressive contour, his method of building up a picture by comparatively large areas of unified colour, owe an obvious debt to the Japanese. The high angle of vision adopted by some other painters is obviously derived from the same source, and their habit of allowing one or more of the principal personages in their pictures to be cut in two by the frame—a peculiarity which had never been seen before in European painting—was due partly to the study of photographic snapshots and partly to a purely accidental detail of Japanese colour print production. For convenience of working, Japanese colour prints were frequently produced as *triptychs*. The design spread over the whole composition, but the wood cutting and printing was divided into three sections, and prints from these separate sections frequently came into the hands of Western students in single sheets. This at least seems as plausible an explanation as any for the revolutionary practice adopted by some European painters.

Great as was the influence of the Japanese colour print on design, its effect on subject-matter was no less striking. Japanese connoisseurs themselves did not admire the colour prints; they admired 'ideal' painting, rather like their European counterparts. The colour print to them was so much journalism; interesting no doubt to the vulgar mind but unworthy of the attention of high aesthetic intelligences. Its productions were called *Ukiyoye*—The Mirror of the Passing Show—but the excited Western discoverers of the Japanese print were not likely to know this, and to them it was a revelation, an opening of doors on unlimited new possibilities in painting. For if the Japanese had succeeded in producing this curiously satisfying Art merely by looking around them and drawing what they saw,

51

setting it down as by a rapid notation without any undue concessions to naturalism; conscious chiefly of its topical interest, but endowing it half unconsciously with such pronounced decorative qualities, surely it was possible to look around one in contemporary Paris and set down what one saw with the same freedom of line, the same gaiety of colour, and the same expressive arabesque. Such at least seems to the present writer the chief importance of the Japanese revelation.

By our concentration on easel-painting we are apt to forget that the French had had—throughout the nineteenth century and before, back to Abraham Bosse and beyond him to Callot—their own *Ukiyoye*, their Mirror of the Passing Show. The tradition had been a strong one, shared alike by the producers of *Estampes Galantes* and the political cartoonists. The invention of lithography had given it another urge forward, and the whole contents of the early nineteenth-century print shops—among the most frequented shops in Paris in the days when the illustrated newspaper was still a rarity—ranging from sugary fashion plates to savage caricatures, had been nothing but 'a mirror of the passing show.' Much of this material was no doubt aesthetically negligible, but every now and then an artist emerged who towered above his fellows as Hokusai towers above the other Japanese designers of colour prints. If pictorial journalism and caricature produced in Japan a Hokusai and a Hiroshige, it produced in France a Daumier and a Constantin Guys. Of course, neither of these two men used Japanese methods, the architectural light and shade of Daumier being almost the exact antithesis of the Oriental practice, but their example reinforced the tendency we have been discussing, the willingness to regard contemporary life as legitimate subject-matter for Art.

Other effects must be noted in passing. No doubt Millet's peasants were contemporary, but they were remote, intentionally remote, from the appetites and interests of the ordinary spectator of pictures. In a manner of speaking, they were as exotic and strange as David's Roman heroes, or Delacroix' Near Eastern Pashas; but now French artists, inspired by the practice of the Japanese and fortified by the example of the French illustrators, turned to the real life about them, which, in most cases, meant the life of great cities. When they specialized, they specialized in the

E. Degas 47 "LE VICOMTE LEPIC" M. Gerstenberg

Japanese manner, on the life of theatres, or even of *maisons closes*. Gavarni had depicted the humour and bitterness of the life of the *coulisses*. Now Degas was to make of the painted artificiality of the scene a new reality, almost painfully real in its utter absence of sentimentality, but redeemed by an enchantment of colour and an intoxication of design which also was derived largely from the Japanese.

Places of public amusement in Paris had long existed, but towards the end of the century they seemed to take on a new animation. The rise of Montmartre was a revolution in the history of *mœurs*. For Montmartre was not only the scene of a gaiety not yet organized out of existence, but was also a genuine artistic quarter when such quarters were not the shoddy fakes they have since become. The French habit of amusing oneself in public, of eating in restaurants, of meeting one's friends not in clubs but in cafés, very much facilitated the task of the artist who wished to depict contemporary life. The mirror could hardly help reflecting a passing show more animated and brightly coloured than would have been possible anywhere else in Europe.

The opportunity was seized, as we have seen, by Degas, but it was exploited to its full by Toulouse-Lautrec, who began his characteristic work in Paris at the end of the 'eighties. It was the great days of the *Moulin Rouge* and the *Moulin de la Galette*, of *la Goulue* and Jane Avril, of Yvette Guilbert and *Nini Patte-en-l'Air*. Toulouse-Lautrec became as familiar with every aspect of Parisian night life as if he had been himself a cabaret performer or a tout for a *maison close*.

If it is the mark of a great artist to care only for the architectonics of his picture and nothing for its human content, if he should see human beings as so many pieces of cheese, be attentive only to light and shade and harmony of colour, if he should make no sacrifice to representation, in case by doing so something should be stolen from Art, Toulouse-Lautrec was one of the worst painters that ever lived. Yet few even of our aesthetic puritans would be so hardy as to maintain such an opinion, for Toulouse-Lautrec's powers of composition were extraordinary, his line almost miraculously expressive, his colour vivid and yet inevitably harmonious. He is the complete reincarnation of an *Ukiyoye* artist, astray once more in an

K   53

Occidental *Yoshiwara*. He remains one of the greatest pictorial journalists of all time—and how much more!

Renoir is one of the greatest artists and the most attractive painters of the nineteenth century, yet he is most difficult to fit into any of the categories we have been discussing. His technique has affinities with that of Monet as well as with Degas and Manet. Having been for a while under the influence of the followers of Delacroix, he adopted the treble palette typical of the Impressionists, and for a time was almost a *pointilliste*, but he loved also to use the palette knife and to model in a kind of enamel paste, especially in the construction of his nude figures. He spent his early years of poverty as a painter in a porcelain factory, and a hint of the decorative touch he learned there persists even in some of his most mature paintings.

There was nothing of the dogmatism of some of the later Impressionists in Renoir; nothing even of the slightly doctrinaire and fighting spirit of a Manet. He was content to paint for the *volupté de peindre*, and in the process of doing so managed to sum up in his own way the achievement not only of the Impressionists but of the Classicists and the eighteenth-century *genre* painters as well. Not for him the 'scientific' painting of light, the willingness to allow contours to be lost in atmosphere. He was as much fascinated by the arabesque as Ingres himself. He traced the silhouette with obvious pleasure, but it was not the empty silhouette of the Academic painters; it was the silhouette which expressed the interior modelling and the curving over of the planes at the edge of the figure. His *Baigneuses* is a *Bain Turc* come suddenly to life; the figures, brought out from the harem—or the studio—are set in the sunlight, no longer cold abstractions but vivid, human, warm.

Sometimes he seems more like Boucher with his light-blues and pinks and pearly flesh; like him also in a kind of innocent sensuality which, because it is so intimately connected with the actual process of painting, never strikes the spectator as incongruous, or allows him to separate in his own mind manner and matter. At times he seems deliberately to flout all the doctrines of Impressionism. He continually prettifies and idealizes, only, and this is perhaps the important point, he does not do so in response

48　THE GIRL WITH THE SEAGULLS

G. Courbet

M. Paul Rosenberg

49 "LA TOILETTE DE LA MARIÉE"

G. Courbet
Smith College Museum of Art, Massachusetts

50 PORTRAIT OF BAUDELAIRE

G. Courbet
Musée de Montpellier

to any system of studio rules, but in obedience to his own extremely personal
vision. Renoir, indeed, has a natural lyrical quality in all his paintings
which enables him to skate over the thinnest of thin ice, to paint voluptu-
ously without ever falling into eroticism, to paint the subjects which appealed
to him as beautiful in actual life—girls, nude bodies, flowers—and yet
never to fall into the vice of subject, of thinking the beauty of the object
sufficient to justify the picture. He came at moments within a hair's-
breadth of the chocolate box, and was saved from it and all that the phrase
implies, not so much by any conscious dexterity, but by the sheer simplicity
and honesty of his vision. Renoir, in spite of his early struggles, was
probably the most fortunate painter that ever lived. There are those who
can only take the Kingdom of Heaven by violence; Renoir entered it un-
hindered with the assurance of a child. But the childlike quality was in
his spirit only; technically he was one of the most accomplished painters
of the nineteenth century, or indeed of the whole course of French painting.
Having absorbed and forgotten the doctrines of the Impressionists, he was
able to combine them with what he had learned from the painters of previous
Ages and to produce by their aid a completely unified and intensely personal
ideal.

NOTES ON ARTISTS AND PICTURES

COURBET, JEAN-DÉSIRÉ-GUSTAVE
1819–1877

Gustave Courbet was born in the village of Ornans in 1819, the son of a well-to-do farmer. Of independent disposition from childhood, he ignored his father's wish that he should become a lawyer and in 1840 went to Paris, intent on making a career as a painter. Already at the age of twenty-three he had produced as mature a work as 'Courbet au Chien Noir' (Petit Palais), which was exhibited at the Salon of 1844. In 1849 the jury of the Salon awarded him a medal for 'Une Après-Midi à Ornans' (Musée de Lille), but he failed to have either 'L'Enterrement à Ornans' or 'L'Atelier' (both in the Louvre) accepted at the International Exhibition of 1855. Outraged by this rejection, Courbet hurriedly erected a tent in the Avenue Montaigne, called it '*Le Pavillon du Réalisme*,' and held there a personal show of some forty of his works, including the two rejected pictures. The failure of this exhibition to attract the attention of the public did not prevent Courbet from holding a similar and equally unsuccessful opposition show during the Great Exhibition of 1867. By that time he was already becoming closely involved in the activities of the Socialist party, and in 1871, after the fall of Napoleon III, he was made a deputy of the Commune and President of the Federation of Artists. In his revolutionary enthusiasm he demanded the destruction of the Colonne Vendôme, which was pulled down by the mob shortly before order was restored by the National Assembly. The Assembly held Courbet responsible for this act. He was sentenced to six months' imprisonment and ordered to pay 323,091 francs 68 centimes for the restoration of the column. Being quite unable to produce this sum, Courbet decided to leave his native country and in 1873 fled to Switzerland, where he died at La-Tour-de-Peilz, near Vevey, in 1877.

45. THE SLEEPING BATHER.

      Oil on canvas, $35 \times 26\frac{1}{2}$ inches.

Painted in 1845.

Signed.

Coll.: *M. Paul Rosenberg, Paris.*

48. THE GIRL WITH THE SEAGULLS.

      Oil on canvas, $32 \times 25\frac{3}{4}$ inches.

Painted at Deauville in 1865.

Signed: *G. Courbet.*

Formerly in the Benoche collection.

Coll.: *M. Paul Rosenberg, Paris.*

49. LA TOILETTE DE LA MARIÉE.

      Oil on canvas, $73 \times 94\frac{1}{4}$ inches.

Painted about 1864.

Formerly the property of M. Paul Rosenberg, Paris.

Coll.: *Smith College, Massachusetts.*

50. PORTRAIT OF BAUDELAIRE.

      Oil on canvas, $20\frac{7}{8} \times 24$ inches.

The portrait was painted in 1848, when Baudelaire was twenty-seven years of age. It remained in the artist's studio until 1859, when it was bought for 500 francs by the publisher Poulet-Malassis, from whom it was acquired in 1874 by Courbet's friend Alfred Bruyas for 3000 francs. It was left by him to the Museum with the rest of his collection.

Signed: *G. Courbet.*

Coll.: *Musée de Montpellier.*

51. THE TALLY-HO! (*L'Hallali du Chevreuil.*)

      Oil on canvas, $81\frac{1}{2} \times 128$ inches.

Painted in 1858 during the artist's stay at Frankfurt.

Signed: *G. Courbet.*

Coll.: *The Wallraf-Richartz Museum, Cologne.*

DAUMIER, HONORÉ
1808–1879

Honoré Daumier was born at Marseilles in 1808, the son of a glazier who had written a book of poems. In 1814 the Daumiers took up residence in Paris, where young Honoré was successively given employment by a

G. Courbet

51   THE TALLY-HO!

The Wallraf-Richartz Museum, Cologne

52   THE PICTURE-LOVERS

H. Daumier

M. Paul Rosenberg

bailiff, a notary and a bookseller. He spent his spare time making drawings in the Louvre, eventually attracting the attention of Alexandre Lenoir, the founder of the Musée des Monuments Français, and was sent to a certain Ramelet to study lithography. In 1830 he began to contribute political cartoons to a paper called *Caricature*, and in 1832 had to spend six months in prison for a representation of Louis-Philippe as 'Gargantua swallowing bags of gold extorted from the people.' On his release Daumier went on working for *Caricature* until its final suspension in 1835. He then joined *Charivari*. In 1860 his eyesight began to fail. Ten years later he became totally blind, and would have died completely destitute if his friend Corot had not helped him and given him a house at Valmondois-sur-Seine-et-Oise, where he lived till his death in 1879.

As a painter, Daumier was disregarded by his contemporaries, who considered him merely a caricaturist. Yet his paintings were accepted in the Salon four times: in 1849, 1851, 1861 and 1869.

1. THE PRINT-LOVER.
   Oil on canvas, 14×10 inches.
   Signed.
   Formerly the property of Georges Viau, Paris.
   Coll.: *Sir William Burrell, Berwick-on-Tweed.*

46. THE PICTURE STALL.
   Oil on canvas, $12\frac{3}{4} \times 9\frac{3}{4}$ inches.
   Painted about 1855.
   Signed.
   Remained from 1860 to 1917 in the Lemaire collection.
   Coll.: *Mme. Emil Staub-Terlinden, Männedorf, Switzerland.*

52. THE PICTURE-LOVERS.
   Oil on canvas, $15\frac{3}{4} \times 12\frac{1}{2}$ inches.
   Signed.
   Former collections: Comte de Camondo; Georges Feydeau; Joubert Cronier; W. Blumenthal; Édouard Jonas.
   Coll.: *M. Paul Rosenberg, Paris.*

54. AT THE THEATRE.
   Oil sketch on canvas, $10\frac{5}{8} \times 13\frac{3}{4}$ inches.
   Coll.: *Baron Robert von Hirsch, Basle.*

55. THE CHESS-PLAYERS.

Oil on canvas, $19\frac{1}{2} \times 13\frac{7}{8}$ inches.

Painted in 1868.

Signed.

Formerly the property of M. Jacquette, who bequeathed it to the Museum of the city of Paris.

Coll.: *Le Petit Palais, Paris.*

MILLET, JEAN-FRANÇOIS

1814–1875

Millet was born in 1814 at the hamlet of Gruchy, near Cherbourg. He was of peasant stock, and spent his childhood on his parents' farm. His aptitude for drawing manifested itself early, and in 1832 he was sent to Cherbourg to study with Langlois. In 1837 he went to Paris, where he became a pupil of Paul Delaroche. But he did not get on with his master and soon left him. For the next ten years he lived alternately in Paris and at Cherbourg, where he painted portraits and where he married first in 1841, and, on the death of his wife, again in 1844. With his second wife he went to Le Havre, where an exhibition of his works had a great success. In 1845 he returned to Paris, where he stayed till 1849, when the then raging epidemic of cholera decided him to take up residence at Barbizon. It was here that he produced all his most famous pictures, such as 'Le Semeur' (Mrs. W. H. Vanderbilt, New York), 'L'Angélus' (Louvre) and 'Les Glaneuses' (Louvre). At the International Exhibition of 1867 he was awarded a first-class medal and in the next year received the Legion of Honour. In 1873 he was commissioned by the Government to decorate a part of the Panthéon, but owing to failing health was unable to execute this work. He died at Barbizon in 1875.

56. THE WOOD-GATHERERS. (*Les Bûcheronnes.*)

Oil on canvas, $32\frac{3}{8} \times 39\frac{1}{2}$ inches.

Unsigned, but bears the stamp of the Millet Sale in 1875.

Formerly in the collection of Henri Rouart, Paris.

Coll.: *Miss G. E. Davies, Montgomery.*

53 "LA SERVEUSE DE BOCKS"

E. Manet

The National Gallery, Millbank

TISSOT, JAMES-JOSEPH-JACQUES
1836–1902

James Tissot was born at Nantes in 1836. He studied at the École des Beaux-Arts in Paris under Flandrin, Lamothe and Ingres, and met with early success when his first exhibit at the Salon of 1861—'Faust et Marguerite' (Louvre)—was purchased by the State. He first exhibited at the Royal Academy in 1864. During the Franco-Prussian War he took part in the defence of Paris. In 1872 he established himself in London, where he was highly esteemed as a painter and where for several years he was a popular figure in society. But a love affair with a married woman, who appears in many of his pictures, made him give up social life and lead a secluded existence in his St. John's Wood home. After his mistress's death in 1882 he left London and returned to Paris. In 1886 he visited Palestine, and devoted the rest of his life to illustrating the New Testament and the Bible. His drawings for 'The Life of Christ' were a huge success: people crowded to see them when they were exhibited at the Louvre and a publisher paid him a million francs for them. The series of illustrations for the Bible, the completion of which was interrupted by his death, was never published and is now lost. Tissot died at Nantes in 1902.

57. A ROOM BOMBARDED DURING THE SIEGE OF PARIS.
    Oil on canvas, 12½×16 inches.
  Painted in 1871.
  Coll.: *The Leicester Galleries, London.*

MANET, ÉDOUARD
1832–1883

Manet was born in Paris in 1832. His parents, who belonged to the higher *bourgeoisie*, did not approve of their son becoming an artist and wanted him to study law. But Manet refused to do so and chose rather to go to sea. After a year in the mercantile marine he managed to overcome his parents' objections and in 1850 entered the studio of Couture, where, in spite of continual dissensions and rows with the master, he remained for

L   61 five years. During that period he met Mlle. Leenhoff, a Dutch woman, from whom he took piano lessons and who became his mistress and, in 1863, his wife. He first participated at the Salon in 1861 with 'Le Chanteur Espagnol' (coll. Osborn, New York) and the 'Portrait of M. and Mme. Auguste Manet' (coll. Rouart, Paris), but in 1863 the jury rejected 'Le Déjeuner sur l'Herbe' (Louvre). The picture was exhibited instead at the Salon des Refusés, where it roused a storm of indignation. In 1865 'Olympia' (Louvre), though hung in the official Salon, caused another scandal. In the same year Manet visited Spain, though most of the pictures of his so-called 'Spanish Period' were painted before this journey, in Paris. In 1867, not having been invited to participate in the International Exhibition, he installed himself, like Courbet, in a shed near the Pont de l'Alma, where he showed some fifty of his works. None were sold, and although he was sponsored by various critics, Émile Zola and Théodore Duret among them, the lack of public appreciation continued for many years. After the Franco-Prussian War, during which he served in the *Garde Nationale*, he came into touch with the Impressionists, and took part in their exhibitions, continuing at the same time to send to the Salons, where his pictures were accepted one year and refused the next. It was not until 1881 that 'Pertuiset Chasseur de Lions' (coll. Mme. Durieux, Abbazia) was awarded a medal which gave Manet the right to exhibit his works without submitting them to the jury. But by that time his health had begun to give way, and he died in Paris in 1883 from gangrene which set in after the amputation of a leg.

53. 'LA SERVEUSE DE BOCKS.'
> Oil on canvas, $38\frac{1}{2} \times 31$ inches.

The scene takes place in the *Brasserie de Reichshoffen*, a cabaret in the Boulevard Rochechourd.

> Signed: *Manet*, and dated: 79.
> Another version of the same subject is in the possession of Baron Matsukata, Tokio.
> Former collections: Manet sale, 1884; Haviland.
> Presented to the Gallery by the Trustees of the Courtauld Fund in 1924.
> Coll.: *The National Gallery, Millbank, London.*

58. PORTRAIT OF PERTUISET, THE LION-HUNTER.
> Oil on canvas, $58\frac{7}{8} \times 66\frac{3}{4}$ inches.

54   AT THE THEATRE

H. Daumier   *Baron R. von Hirsch*

55   THE CHESS-PLAYERS

H. Daumier   *Le Petit Palais, Paris*

56   THE WOOD-GATHERERS

J. F. Millet   *Miss G. E. Davies*

57   A ROOM BOMBARDED DURING THE SIEGE OF PARIS

J. Tissot   *The Leicester Galleries, London*

Pertuiset was a famous big-game hunter. The landscape was painted in the garden of his house at 14, Passage de l'Élysée-des-Beaux-Arts in Montmartre.

First exhibited at the Salon in 1881, where it was awarded a second medal.

Signed: *Manet*, and dated: *1881*.

Former collections: Pertuiset, Paris; Gerstenberg, Grünewald-Berlin; Silberberg, Breslau.

Coll.: *Mme. Tilla Durieux, Abbazia, Italy.*

59. ARGENTEUIL.

Oil on canvas, $58\frac{1}{2} \times 51\frac{1}{2}$ inches.

The gentleman in the picture is Rodolphe Leenhoff, Manet's brother-in-law.

Signed: *Manet*, and dated: *1874*.

First exhibited at the Salon in 1875.

Former collections: Manet Sale, 1884, bought in by the family for 12,500 francs; sold by Mme. Manet in 1889 for 14,000 francs to Henri van Cutsem, who left it to Guillaume Charlier; bequeathed by the latter to the Museum.

Coll.: *Musée des Beaux-Arts, Tournai.*

60. A BULL FIGHT.

Oil on canvas, $35 \times 43\frac{1}{2}$ inches.

Painted in 1866 in Paris, after the artist's return from Spain.

Purchased from the artist by Pertuiset; sold at his sale in 1888 for 4000 francs. From 1895 in the Durand-Ruel collection.

Coll.: *Baronne Goldschmidt-Rothschild.*

61. A HOUSE AT RUEIL.

Oil on canvas, $28\frac{5}{8} \times 36\frac{1}{8}$ inches.

The house belonged to the playwright Labiche and was inhabited by Manet during the summer. An oblong replica of the picture is in the Melbourne Museum.

Painted in 1882.

Coll.: *National Gallerie, Berlin.*

62. A BOY WITH A DOG.

Oil on canvas, $36 \times 28\frac{1}{2}$ inches.

Painted in 1862.

Signed.

Former collections: Lambert, Nice; de Yourbe, Paris; Mme. A. Rosenberg; Mme. Bohringer, Mannheim; Dr. Reber, Lausanne; Stransky, New York.

Coll.: *Baronne Goldschmidt-Rothschild.*

63. PORTRAIT OF MADAME MANET.

Oil on canvas, $23\frac{3}{4} \times 20$ inches.

Painted about 1868.

Signed.

From the collection of George Moore, who bought it from the artist.

Coll.: *Lady Cunard, London.*

64. BERTHE MORISOT WITH A MUFF.

Oil on canvas, $28\frac{3}{4} \times 23\frac{3}{4}$ inches.

Painted about 1869. One of several portraits which Manet did of Berthe Morisot, the artist, who married his brother Eugène in 1874.

Former collections: Manet sale, 1884; Aug. Pellerin, Paris; Jules Strauss, Paris.

Coll.: *Colonel and Mme. Balsan, Paris.*

65. MADAME MANET IN THE GREENHOUSE.

Oil on canvas, $31\frac{1}{2} \times 39\frac{7}{8}$ inches.

Manet did two pictures of the same subject. Painted between 1876 and 1878 in the artist's studio in Paris.

Signed.

Sold by Mme. Manet to M. Joyant in 1895.

Acquired by the Oslo Gallery in 1918.

Coll.: *National Gallery, Oslo.*

98. FLOWERS.

Oil on canvas, $21\frac{1}{8} \times 13\frac{1}{4}$ inches.

Signed in monogram: *É. M.*

Former collections: Auguste Pellerin, Paris; W. Hansen, Copenhagen.

Coll.: *Dr. Oskar Reinhart, Winterthur, Switzerland.*

BAZILLE, JEAN-FRÉDERIC
1841–1870

Bazille was born in Montpellier in 1841. He was a pupil of Gleyre, in whose studio he met and became friends with Renoir, Monet and Sisley. He first exhibited at the Salon in 1866. His promising artistic career was cut short in 1870, when he was killed in action at the battle of Beaune-la-Rolande.

66. THE ARTIST'S STUDIO.

Oil on canvas, $38\frac{1}{8} \times 50$ inches.

58   PORTRAIT OF PERTUISET, THE LION-HUNTER

E. Manet

Madame Tilla Durieux

59 ARGENTEUIL

E. Manet

Musée des Beaux-Arts, Tournai

60 A BULL FIGHT

E. Manet   *Baronne Goldschmidt-Rothschild*

61 A HOUSE AT RUEIL

E. Manet   *National Gallerie, Berlin*

62 A BOY WITH A DOG

E. Manet

Baronne Goldschmidt-Rothschild

The figure of Bazille in the centre of the picture was painted by Manet. The other personages are Manet, Monet, Renoir, Edmond Maître, and probably Zola.

Signed: *F. Bazille*, and dated: *1870*.

Coll.: *Musée du Louvre, Paris*.

DEGAS, EDGAR-HILAIRE-GERMAIN

1834–1917

Degas was born in Paris in 1834. His father was a French banker and his mother a Creole from New Orleans. Though he spent only one year at the École des Beaux-Arts, his early work was wholly in the classical academic tradition. He exhibited at the Salons and led the existence of a wealthy young man-about-town, frequenting fashionable *rendezvous*, race-courses and theatres. It was not until after the Franco-Prussian War, in which he took an active part, that he began to frequent the more bohemian resorts of Paris. At the Café Guerbois in the Avenue de Clichy and '*La Nouvelle Athènes*' in the Batignolles quarter he met Manet, Renoir and the other Impressionists, and, ceasing to exhibit at the official Salons, became a contributor to the shows organized by their opposition group. But gradually his relations with the Impressionists became more and more strained, and in 1886 he ceased to exhibit with them or anywhere else. From then on he led the life of a recluse, seeing practically no one and disposing of his pictures through Durand-Ruel, with whom he had a contract. After 1890 he gave up painting in oil and produced only pastels. He died in Paris in 1917.

47. 'LE VICOMTE LEPIC.'

Oil on canvas, $31 \times 46\frac{3}{8}$ inches.

The Viscount Lepic was an engraver. He is here represented crossing the Place de la Concorde with his two daughters.

Painted in 1873-74.

Coll.: *M. Gerstenberg, Berlin*.

67. PORTRAIT OF THE ARTIST.

Oil on canvas, $35\frac{3}{8} \times 24\frac{3}{8}$ inches.

Painted about 1864. Remained in the artist's possession until his death.

Coll.: *Mlle. Fèvre, Paris*.

68. BALLET SCENE FROM 'ROBERTO IL DIAVOLO.'
        Oil on canvas, $26 \times 21\frac{5}{8}$ inches.
    Signed: *Degas*, and dated: *1872*.
    From the Constantine A. Ionides collection, which was bequeathed to the Museum.
    Coll.: *Victoria and Albert Museum, London.*

69. WOMEN COMBING THEIR HAIR.
        Oil on canvas, $13 \times 18\frac{1}{2}$ inches.
    Sometimes also referred to as 'La Toilette sur la Plage.'
    Painted about 1876.
    Signed.
    Coll.: *M. Guillaume Lerolle, Paris.*

70. TWO DANCERS ON THE STAGE.
        Oil on canvas, $24\frac{1}{4} \times 18\frac{1}{4}$ inches.
    Painted about 1877.
    Signed.
    Former collections: Gallimard; Sir James Murray; Knoedler; Samuel Courtauld.
    Coll.: *Courtauld Institute of Art, London.*

71. DANCERS AT EXERCISE.
        Oil on canvas, $10\frac{1}{2} \times 8\frac{1}{4}$ inches.
    Painted about 1878.
    Signed.
    Formerly in the collection of Henri Rouart, Paris.
    Coll.: *Comtesse de Béhague, Paris.*

72. JOCKEYS. (*Les Courses.*)
        Oil on panel, $10\frac{5}{8} \times 13\frac{3}{4}$ inches.
    Painted in 1885.
    Signed.
    Coll.: *M. Guillaume Lerolle, Paris.*

73. PORTRAIT OF MADAME JEANTAUD.
        Oil on canvas, $27\frac{3}{4} \times 33\frac{1}{4}$ inches.
    Mme. Jeantaud was the wife of an engineer and a friend of the artist.
    The picture has also been called '*La Dame au Miroir.*'
    Painted about 1874.
    Signed.
    Coll.: *Mme. Jacques Doucet, Paris.*

64 BERTHE MORISOT WITH A MUFF

Colonel and Madame Balsan

E. Manet

63 PORTRAIT OF MADAME MANET

Lady Cunard

E. Manet

65   MADAME MANET IN THE GREENHOUSE

E. Manet

74. THE BEACH. (*La Plage.*)

Oil on canvas, 18×32½ inches.

Signed.

Former collections: Henri Rouart, Paris; Sir Hugh Lane.

Coll.: *The National Gallery, Millbank, London.*

75. WOMEN IRONING.

Oil on canvas, 32½×29½ inches.

Painted in 1882.

Signed.

Another version of the same subject, similar in composition but differing in detail, is in the Durand-Ruel collection in Paris. Formerly in the collection of Oskar Schmitz, Dresden (catalogued under the title: *Les Blanchisseuses*).

Coll.: *M. Georges Wildenstein, Paris.*

76. THE RACES AT LONGCHAMPS.

Oil on canvas, 18¼×25⅛ inches.

Painted in 1869.

Signed.

Formerly in the collection Holzmann, Berlin.

Coll.: *Baron Robert von Hirsch, Basle.*

TOULOUSE-LAUTREC, HENRI DE
1864–1901

Henri de Toulouse-Lautrec was born at Albi in 1864, and was a direct descendant of the Comtes de Toulouse. As a child he had two accidents, both his legs were fractured and he was left a dwarf and a cripple for life. In 1882 he went to Paris, where he studied first under Bonnat and then under Cormon. When he finished his apprenticeship he installed himself in Montmartre, where he painted indefatigably all day pictures of the Parisian night-life in which he avidly partook. He paid several visits to London, where he met Whistler, Conder and Wilde (of whom he made a coloured drawing) and where in 1898 he held an exhibition at the Goupil Gallery. If his paintings were not much appreciated during his lifetime, his lithographs and posters had a considerable success. Towards the end of his life, owing to his long indulgence in drink, his health began to suffer, and in

1899 he had to spend ten weeks in a mental home. Nevertheless his creative capacities remained unaffected, and he went on working until a short time before his death, which occurred at the Château de Malromé, Gironde, in 1901.

77. DANCERS AT THE MOULIN ROUGE.
  Oil on canvas, $36\frac{1}{2} \times 31\frac{1}{2}$ inches.
  Painted in 1892.
  Coll.: *Gallery of Modern Art, Prague.*

78. 'LA CLOWNESS.'
  Oil on canvas, $31\frac{2}{3} \times 25$ inches.
  The scene represents the Moulin Rouge; the central figure is the clowness Cha-U-Kao, with the dancer Gabrielle on her right and the playwright Tristan Bernard in the background on his left.
  Signed: *Lautrec*, and dated: *1895.*
  The picture was bought from the artist by King Milan of Serbia, after whose assassination it was sold with his other pictures and acquired by M. Bernheim, jeune.
  Coll.: *Dr. Oskar Reinhart, Winterthur, Switzerland.*

79. 'CHILPÉRIC.'
  Oil on canvas, 59×57 inches.
  Painted in 1895. The subject is a scene from Hervé's operetta 'Chilpéric,' which was revived that year at the Théâtre des Variétés in Paris. Mlle. Marcelle Lender is seen executing the 'Pas de Boléro.' Among the other actors are de Lassouche (seated), Vauthier, Brasseur fils, Baron, Mlle. Diéterle and Simon (standing on right).
  Signed: *T. L.*
  Formerly in the collection of M. Joyant.
  Coll.: *Mme. Dortu, Le Vesinet, France.*

80. THE TOILET.
  Oil on cardboard, $29 \times 25\frac{3}{4}$ inches.
  Painted in 1891.
  Signed: *T. Lautrec.*
  Former collections: Depeaux; Mme. Besnard; Sevadijan; Gerald Brooks.
  Coll.: *Mrs. Chester Beatty, London.*

81. JANE AVRIL.
  Gouache and pastel millboard, 39×21 inches.

F. Bazille 1870

J. F. Bazille   66   THE ARTIST'S STUDIO   *Musée du Louvre, Paris*

67 PORTRAIT OF THE ARTIST

E. Degas

Mademoiselle Fèvre

68   BALLET SCENE FROM "ROBERTO IL DIAVOLO"

E. Degas   *Victoria & Albert Museum, London*

69   WOMEN COMBING THEIR HAIR

E. Degas   *M. G. Lerolle*

70 TWO DANCERS ON THE STAGE

E. Degas

The Courtauld Institute of Art, London

71 DANCERS AT EXERCISE

E. Degas

Comtesse de Béhague

72   JOCKEYS

E. Degas   *M. G. Lerolle*

73   PORTRAIT OF MADAME JEANTAUD

E. Degas   *Madame Jacques Doucet*

74 THE BEACH

E. Degas   *The National Gallery, Millbank*

75 WOMEN IRONING

E. Degas   *M. Georges Wildenstein*

Baron R. von Hirsch

76   THE RACES AT LONGCHAMPS

E. Degas

78 "LA CLOWNESSE"

Dr. O. Reinhart

H. de Toulouse-Lautrec

77 DANCERS AT THE MOULIN ROUGE

Gallery of Modern Art, Prague

H. de Toulouse-Lautrec

79   "CHILPÉRIC"

H. de Toulouse-Lautrec   *Madame Dortu*

80   THE TOILET

H. de Toulouse-Lautrec

Mrs. Chester Beatty

Jane Avril was a dancer at the Moulin Rouge.
Signed: *T. Lautrec*.
Former collections: Prince Murat; Blot; Pridonoff.
Coll.: *The Courtauld Institute of Art, London*.

RENOIR, PIERRE-AUGUSTE

1841–1919

Renoir, who was the son of a tailor, was born at Limoges in 1841. Shortly afterwards his parents moved to Paris, where at the age of thirteen he started earning his living, first as a china decorator at a porcelain factory, then as a painter of fans and window blinds. In 1862 he had saved up enough money to enable him to enter the studio of Gleyre. Here he met and made friends with Monet, Sisley and Bazille. The pictures which he submitted to the jury of the Salon were more often rejected than accepted. He took part in the Impressionist exhibitions of 1874 and 1877. In 1880 he married, and in the same year went to Italy, visiting Venice, Rome, Naples and Palermo. By that time he was beginning to be seriously troubled by rheumatic gout, and with a view to benefiting his health spent in 1882 some time in Algiers. The next twenty-five years he resided in Paris, travelling a good deal during the summer months. In 1907 he bought a property at Cagnes on the Côte d'Azur, where he lived until his death in 1919. Towards the end of his life he was so crippled by rheumatism that he was unable to hold his brushes, and they had to be tied to his fingers so as to enable him to paint.

44. THE CONCERT.
    Oil on canvas, $36\frac{1}{4} \times 28\frac{3}{4}$ inches.
    Painted in 1919, shortly before the artist's death.
    Coll.: *M. Claude Renoir, Paris*.

82. A WINTER DAY IN THE BOIS DE BOULOGNE.
    Oil on canvas, $28\frac{3}{8} \times 35\frac{3}{8}$ inches.
    Signed: *A. Renoir*, and dated: *68*.
    Coll.: *Baron Robert von Hirsch, Basle*.

M

83. THE HORSEWOMAN. (*L'Amazone.*)
>   Oil on canvas, 29×15 inches.

A study for the painting 'Allée cavalière au Bois de Boulogne' in the Kunsthalle, Hamburg.
>   Painted in 1873.
>   Signed: *A. Renoir.*
>   Formerly in the collection Le Cœur, Paris.
>   Coll.: *Baron Napoléon Gourgaud, Paris.*

84. PORTRAIT OF MLLE. HENRIOT.
>   Oil on canvas, 21¾×18⅛ inches.
>   Signed: *Renoir.*
>   Coll.: *Dr. Oskar Reinhart, Winterthur, Switzerland.*

85. A YOUNG WOMAN AGAINST A BLUE BACKGROUND.
>   Oil on canvas, 26×21½ inches.
>   Painted in 1884.
>   Coll.: *M. Henri Bernstein, Paris.*

86. THE BLONDE BATHER.
>   Oil on canvas, 31½×24¾ inches.

Begun in Naples in 1881 and finished in 1882. A replica of this picture, painted at the same time, is in America. Twice engraved by the artist himself.
>   Signed: *Renoir.*
>   Former collections: Gallimard, Paris; J. B. Stang, Oslo; Alfred Gold, Paris.
>   Coll.: *Kenneth Clark, Esq., London.*

87. A GUST OF WIND.
>   Oil on canvas, 19×31 inches.
>   Painted about 1877.
>   Signed: *A. Renoir.*
>   Coll.: *F. Hindley Smith, Esq., Seaford.*

88. FEEDING THE CHICKENS.
>   Oil on canvas, 23½×28½ inches.
>   Painted in 1879.
>   Signed: *Renoir.*
>   Former collections: Louis Bernard, Paris; Richard Goetz, Paris.
>   Coll.: *Baron Robert de Rothschild, Paris.*

81   JANE AVRIL

H. de Toulouse-Lautrec   *The Courtauld Institute of Art, London*

82   A WINTER DAY IN THE BOIS DE BOULOGNE

A. Renoir

A. Renoir

83 THE HORSEWOMAN

Baron Gourgaud

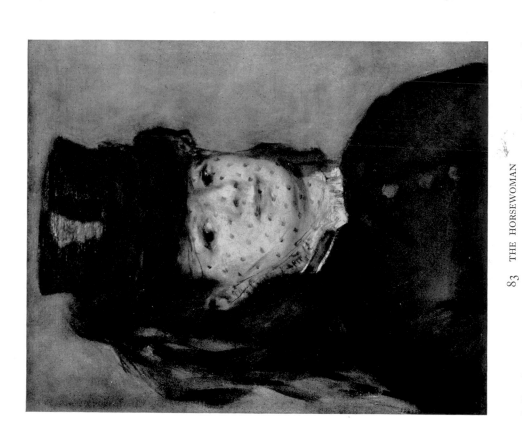

A. Renoir

84 PORTRAIT OF MADEMOISELLE HENRIOT

Dr. O. Reinhart

A. Renoir   85 YOUNG WOMAN AGAINST A BLUE BACKGROUND   *M. Henri Bernstein*

86 THE BLONDE BATHER   *Kenneth Clark, Esq.*   A. Renoir

89. NUDE.

Oil on canvas, $36\frac{1}{4} \times 28\frac{3}{4}$ inches.
The model used for this painting was known as '*la Belle Anna.*'
Signed and dated 1876.
Coll.: *Museum of Modern Western Art, Moscow.*

90. BOY WITH A CAT.

Oil on canvas, $48\frac{3}{4} \times 26\frac{1}{4}$ inches.
Signed: *A. Renoir,* and dated: *68.*
Coll.: *Madame Eduard Arnhold, Berlin.*

91. THE JUDGMENT OF PARIS.

Oil on canvas, $31\frac{7}{8} \times 39\frac{3}{8}$ inches.
The artist's servant Gabrielle, who was often painted by him in his later years, was the model for Paris and the goddess seen from the back. Renoir painted several other versions of the same subject.
Signed: *Renoir,* and dated: *1908.*
Formerly in the collection of Mrs. Halvorsen, Oslo.
Coll.: *Charles Laughton, Esq., London.*

96. PORTRAIT OF VICTOR CHOQUET.

Oil on canvas, $18 \times 14\frac{1}{8}$ inches.
Painted in 1876.
Signed: *Renoir.*
Compare with the portrait of Choquet by Cézanne (fig. 95).
Coll.: *Dr. Oskar Reinhart, Winterthur, Switzerland.*

87 A GUST OF WIND

A. Renoir   *Hindley Smith, Esq.*

88 FEEDING THE CHICKENS

A. Renoir   *Baron R. de Rothschild*

89 NUDE

A. Renoir

Museum of Modern Western Art, Moscow

90　BOY WITH A CAT

A. Renoir

Madame E. Arnhold

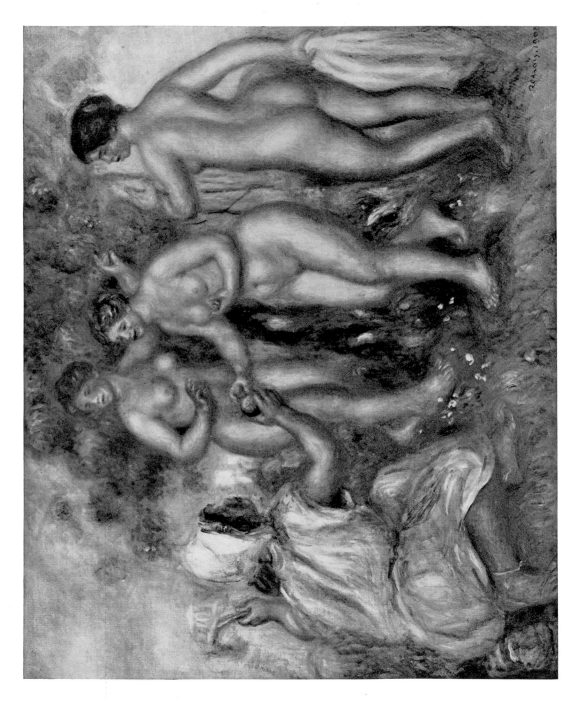

91   THE JUDGEMENT OF PARIS

92 "CÉZANNE CHAUVE"

P. Cézanne

The National Gallery, Millbank

VI

THE TRIUMPH OF SCIENCE

THE second half, or perhaps it would be truer to say the last third of the nineteenth century, saw the rise of a new religion, the Religion of Science. Scientific workers in all fields seemed to have inherited the mantle of both the priest and the prophet. They were the new Popes endowed with a more convincing infallibility, and it really appeared to many educated people that at last all the secrets of the universe would be discovered and all the problems of human life solved. This superstition, which we may for convenience call 'Scientism,' has now been largely exploded. It is seen that science is a method of experimental enquiry within certain rigid limits, and that its results are true only within a narrow field. Science has failed to give us a philosophy, or rather it has approached the possibility of doing so only because the scientists themselves have modified their materialism and abated some of their pretensions. But at the end of the nineteenth century the triumphs of Science were so striking, and its achievements in changing the conditions of life so obvious, that there seemed for a moment as if there were nothing which it could not do. A scientific attitude was born, misunderstood by the majority of people, no doubt, but none the less effective for that, which modified every human activity and every aspect of life. It would have been strange indeed if Art had escaped the general contagion, and in one of its aspects the Impressionist movement is nothing but an attempt to apply to painting the methods of the laboratory.

How could such methods be applied to painting? In theory at least by turning every artist into a kind of research worker into Nature, recording her passing moods, concentrating on effects of light and colour and keeping the personal element as subordinate as possible. Just as Zola and the brothers Goncourt had looked upon their novels as pure documentation, so painters were to look upon their pictures as contributions to the sum of knowledge. They were to work with their eye on the object, to paint in a word their 'impression.' The whole Impressionist School received its name from Monet's '*Impression: Soleil Levant*,' exhibited at the first exhibition of the group in 1874. The name, ridiculed by journalists, caught the fancy of the public, and the artists themselves shortly changed the name of their group from 'Société Anonyme des Artistes, Peintres, Sculpteurs et Graveurs' (a clumsy title at best) to that of 'Peintres Impressionistes.'

To the public and the critics the 'Peintres Impressionistes' formed a homogeneous school, but this was far from being the case in reality, for the group included, in addition to true Impressionists like Boudin, Monet, Sisley and Pissarro, three painters who were greater than any of these and were ultimately among them to upset the Impressionist doctrine—Renoir, Degas and Cézanne. The group did not include Manet, who remained, however, in sympathetic touch with the leaders.

The pure Impressionist doctrine taught that the artist should paint the immediate effect of an object upon his optic nerve, and this is what the leaders of the movement really imagined that they were doing. A moment's reflection, however, will show that this is impossible. The attempt to detach the momentary impression from our general ideas is doomed to failure, for if these general ideas did not exist visual perception itself would be impossible. Monet painted his haystack twelve times in varying conditions of light, and could not avoid, in spite of his theory, a certain generalization and synthesis; and the same is true of Pissarro's paintings of Paris streets. But what the Impressionists did accomplish was to escape from the tyrannies of the studio arrangement. Perhaps all the greatest paintings *are* studio arrangements, but they should not seem so. At least it is desirable that they should not echo other studio arrangements. And the Impressionism certainly introduced a new spontaneity which is none the less real because the theory on which it was based is largely an illusion. The artist came out of the studio and painted in the open air, keeping the sun off his head and the rain out of his colours as best he could.

There is much to be said for *pleinairisme* if only as a method of forcing the eye to observe afresh; but it has obvious disadvantages. The intensity of the light makes it difficult for the artist to get his values correctly, and

93 THE WHITE HORSE

A. Monticelli

Corporation Art Gallery, Glasgow

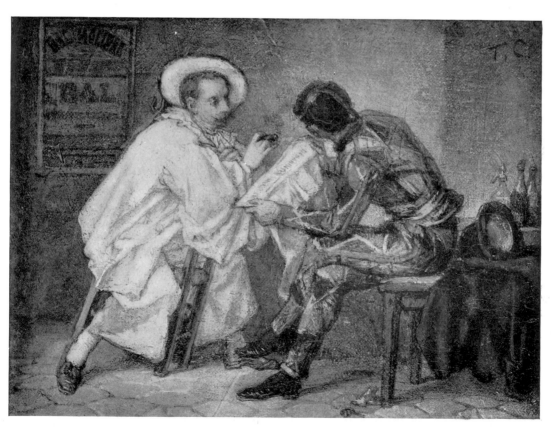

94 HARLEQUIN AND PIERROT

T. Couture

The Wallace Collection, London

P. Cézanne   95   PORTRAIT OF VICTOR CHOQUET   A. Renoir

Victor Rothschild, Esq.

96   PORTRAIT OF VICTOR CHOQUET   *Dr. O. Reinhart*

98 FLOWERS

E. Manet

Dr. O. Reinhart

97 STILL LIFE

H. Fantin-Latour

Musée de Grenoble

99 "LES YEUX CLOS"

O. Redon

Musée du Luxembourg, Paris

a work which looked right in the open air sometimes did not look right when brought indoors to be exhibited in a gallery or hung in a room. Then, too, the intense light soon affected the eyes of the artist. The third objection is that an artist working out of doors is denied many of the effects which are possible to one painting in a studio. His work must of necessity be done *alla prima*, direct on to the canvas.

It is true that Velasquez and Hals had painted in this manner without underpainting or successive glazing. The genius of Velasquez and his infallible instinct for composition enabled him to produce work which has always the repose, the unity and the completeness of pictures constructed on more deliberate methods. But all the *bravura* of Hals does not quite succeed in lifting much of his work above the quality of brilliant sketching. The works of the pure Impressionists are necessarily sketches for the same reason, and the public in the end grew so accustomed to seeing these sketches and accepting them as finished works of art that it was unable to conceive of any other kind of painting. But to refuse to paint any picture which is not a sketch is seriously to limit aesthetic possibilities. The manner involves a drastic simplification, an abandonment of any elaborate composition, and the reduction of painting to a series of *morceaux bien peints*. The followers of the Impressionists are still covering the walls of exhibitions with *morceaux bien peints*, and sometimes not so *bien peints*. The Impressionists' doctrine made composition in the old sense almost impossible.

The answer of the Impressionists would have been that composition as it was understood by the School was artificial and airless of necessity, seeing that it was the Academic practice to make separate studies of all the principal figures and then, as it were, to cut them out and place them arbitrarily on the canvas in accordance with some prearranged design. Such figures, conceived *in vacuo*, never really fitted into the picture at all and could only be made to seem to do so either by *bravura* brushwork, linking the whole composition together, or else by covering the whole canvas when it was finished with a varnish and relying upon its deepening golden tones to obtain the unified effect.

The most important thing in a picture, according to the Impressionist doctrine, was atmosphere, which the Academic painters had neglected altogether. All objects are bathed in and coloured by it. The picture, therefore, is not a representation of objects but of the atmosphere in which they are placed. Atmosphere can only be recorded by studying the effects of light, registering its incidence, recording its vibration, analysing it into the hues of the spectrum, which are present in varying proportions in the apparent colours of all objects. Colour, in short, is something in the eye of the beholder. There is no such thing as 'local' colour, and therefore the work of men like the Pre-Raphaelites, who based their whole practice on an intensity of local colour, is founded on a falsity. Equally false is the Academic practice of treating shadow as the mere opposite of light and of constructing a picture on the basis of *chiaroscuro* and drowning all shadowed objects in a kind of brown sauce. Shadows in nature are not like this at all. They are never opaque, but are always full of reflected colours conditioned by the position of lighted objects round them.

The Impressionists would have nothing to do with the age-long tradition of Art which regards draughtsmanship as the natural basis of painting. There is no such thing as a contour, and therefore drawing is an illusion, an abstraction, useful no doubt in sciences like geometry, but quite out of place in the representation of natural objects. In such representation there should be only volume and planes meeting and passing into each other without any arbitrary linear division.

The Impressionists strove to substitute for drawing pure painting, and in painting they strove for the dissociation of tone. Where the Academic painter mixed blue and yellow on his palette and applied the resulting green to his canvas with one stroke of the brush, the Impressionists applied blue and yellow to the canvas in parallel strokes and left to the eye of the observer the task of recomposition. The result was an astonishing increase of brilliance and a valuable addition to the number of effects— as in the rendering of sunlight, for example — which could be obtained by painting. But it was not this so much that the Impressionists aimed at. They used their separate touches as a means of unifying their pictures, for every portion of a painting contained strokes of the same colour, only in different proportions. The musical titles which Whistler gave to his paintings might with more justice have been applied to those of the Impressionists,

100 "CAMILLE"

C. Monet   *Kunsthalle, Bremen*

C. Monet

101   ST. GERMAIN L'AUXERROIS

National Gallerie, Berlin

who really did paint symphonies in green or orange, but never in black or white.

The dissociation of tone was never Whistler's practice; it was not even Manet's, who even when he painted in the open air mixed his colours on his palette in the traditional manner. The leader of pure Impressionism was Monet, who, founding himself upon the optical discoveries of Helmholtz and Chevreul, elevated the dissociation of tone—which incidentally had been practised to a limited extent by Turner, Delacroix, Monticelli and others—into a deliberate doctrine. But in the eyes of some of his followers even Monet's practice seemed too personal and haphazard to be worthy of a scientific Age. About the year 1885 Signac began to substitute for the instinctive juxtaposition of tone, as practised by Monet, an experiment with colour dots of primary hues and of uniform size.

There was still something of the old Adam in Monet's touches of colour; they could be crowded together to indicate volume, or given a direction which almost hinted that there was after all a line in nature. The new *pointillisme* was entirely free from such reproaches. It had, in theory at least, almost eliminated the artist altogether, for it had reduced him to doing something that a photograph could have done better if only it had then been possible to take photographs in colour. The modern three-colour process reproduction comes very near to what *pointillistes* thought they were aiming at, except, of course, that the human hand could never give the minuteness to be obtained with a closely ruled screen. *Pointillisme* has sometimes a curiously woolly, knitted look, and in the hands of some of its most fanatical exponents form was drowned and lost in a kind of shimmering glow.

It seemed for a moment that the dissociation of tone had led directly to the disintegration of painting, but the validity of art and the necessity of the artist's collaboration was shortly to receive an unexpected vindication. Georges Seurat, the greatest of the *pointillistes* and one of the most important painters of the nineteenth century, was modest enough to think that by working out his system to its logical conclusion he could provide the general public with an infallible technique for painting pictures themselves, forgetting that while the unskilled might follow him in his work of the scientific

o

analysis of colour, they were quite unable to do so in the second part of the process involved in the construction of a work of art—the synthesis of the elements thus obtained into a unified design. That synthesis was necessarily personal, and in Seurat's case intensely so. He saw the danger of pure Impressionism, with its emphasis on accidental effects of light, and, no longer content like some of his colleagues to paint whatever he saw before him, set out to arrange the forms he had found in nature into a deliberately monumental pattern. By so doing he undermined and destroyed the whole Impressionist theory.

Scientific theories of painting do little more as a rule than provide their professors with a kind of private drug, heightening the sensibility and giving the subconscious impulses a central intellectual thread round which to crystallize; but Seurat's theories, or at least his practice, helped to change the whole course of Western painting, for they introduced once more those ideas of deliberate construction in a picture which the Impressionists thought they had abandoned for ever. While the followers of the Impressionists continued to paint as if they were the eyes of so many cameras, selecting nothing, rejecting nothing, but setting down exactly what they saw before them, the main current of French and of European painting had flowed into other channels. Once distortion had been accepted—and all deliberate construction implies distortion by its readiness to alter what the artist sees before him—the way was open for Van Gogh, Gauguin and Cézanne.

The distortion practised by the first of these was of a very individual kind. The dots of primary colour used by the *pointillistes* he elongated into writhing stripes, and used them deliberately not only to intensify his colours but to endow the very forms of objects with an almost painful vitality. The elements of Van Gogh's pictures are so active that only the miracle of his own personal vision could reduce his paintings to unity. In the hands of anyone else his methods would have resulted in a mere writhing chaos.

Gauguin used distortion for more purely decorative ends, which is one of the reasons why he has fallen out of favour with the more fanatical upholders of the modern architectural doctrine of painting; yet his simplification of colour, vivid though it might be, his generalization of outline and his non-naturalistic handling, are obviously the antithesis of Impressionist

78

C. Monet

102   THE CANAL AT SAARDAM

Staedel'sches Kunstinstitut, Frankfurt

103   A VILLAGE BY THE SEINE

A. Sisley

practice. If ever a great school of decorative painting arises again in Europe it will owe much of its impulse, and not a little of its technical approach, to Paul Gauguin.

Cézanne's attempt to reintegrate painting, his construction in depth, his use of colour not for its decorative or local qualities but as part of the formal design, his attempt to construct a watertight space, and all the other elements which constitute his revolution in painting, have been fully dealt with elsewhere and are now familiar to all students of art history. To discuss them further would be out of place in an essay which is concerned less with the philosophy of Art than with the psychology of taste. For our purposes it is sufficient to note that Cézanne foreshadowed not only the development of painting during the next few generations, but the development of world affairs.

It would be fantastic to suggest that he was aware of this; in fact, his strength as a painter was that he cared about nothing in the world but his painting. But such a unity of purpose as his sometimes enables a man to be more in tune with universal currents than the more intellectually inclined. The nineteenth century is the century of individualism in painting and in everything else. The twentieth century, whether we like it or not, is plainly going to be a century of reintegration or final collapse. The mystical unity of life in all its manifestations at any given epoch can never be proved, but it can be sensed in retrospect at least as one senses the unity of a work of art. It is no accident that Poussin and Bossuet were contemporaries, nor that in the time of Jeremy Bentham artists pushed their individualism to grotesque extremes. Is it too fanciful to suggest that the totalitarian state is foreshadowed in the whole approach to painting of a man like Cézanne?

It is, however, no reflection on the greatness of Cézanne to suggest that he has sometimes been praised in terms which seem to imply not only that he was a great painter but that he was almost the only great painter. Who has not heard the adepts of the Higher Æsthetic murmuring to themselves the phrase 'Significant Form,' like so many Oriental sages repeating the mystical word 'Om' until they entered into a state of aesthetic *samadhi* in which it was happily unnecessary to look at any pictures at all? Whatever the philosophers may say, the study of the psychology of taste leads inevitably to a certain scepticism, an unwillingness to believe that any artistic revelation is necessarily the final one. Because Cézanne painted in a certain manner it does not follow that all painting must necessarily be in the same manner to the end of time. Perhaps, standing as he did at the beginning of a universal movement, he was compelled to adopt a certain asceticism which it is possible for the movement to outgrow as it progresses. The first ages of most religions are puritan, but the austerity of the cave in the Thebaïd does not preclude the later possibility of Chartres or even of St. Peter's at Rome. The human interest which Cézanne excluded so rigorously from his paintings is bound to reappear, and it is fanatical to suggest that such a reappearance is necessarily a degeneration. Shut off from the plane of the conscious intelligence, it has indeed already returned in the paintings of the *Surréalistes*, even if the human interest in their work would seem largely the concern of the alienist and the psycho-analyst. This is probably only a passing phase, a sign of frustration, a proof that human emotion has yet to be reintegrated for our contemporaries into the completely satisfying work of art. Whether this be so or not, it is legitimate to plead for a larger toleration in criticism, an abandonment of the idea of pure painting and a willingness to consider the great works of the past by their own standards. There is too much of the atmosphere of the chapel in much modern aesthetic theorizing. Art is not a chapel but a church, a very large church with many chapels, and each Age has its own. Must we pull down the Tudor chantry because we have decided that after all the Norman nave is more admirable? Eclecticism may be fatal to painting, but Catholicity is essential to criticism.

MONTICELLI, ADOLPHE-JOSEPH-THOMAS
1824–1886

Monticelli came of an Italian family established in Marseilles. He was born in that town in 1824 and received there his first lessons in painting from Raymond Aubert. He later went to Paris, where he met and came under the influence of Diaz. In Paris his paintings were highly prized, but in Marseilles, where he returned after the Franco-Prussian War and where he remained to the end of his days, he did not find the same appreciation. Towards the end of his life he was forced to peddle his pictures about and sell them for a few francs apiece. He died in a small furnished room in 1886.

93. THE WHITE HORSE.
    Oil on panel, $15\frac{1}{4} \times 23$ inches.
Formerly the property of Mr. Carfrae Alston.
Coll.: *Corporation Art Gallery, Glasgow.*

COUTURE, THOMAS
1815–1879

Couture was born at Senlis, near Paris, in 1815. He studied under Gros and Paul Delaroche, and won the Prix de Rome in 1837. Ten years later he achieved wide popularity with his large composition 'The Romans of the Decadence,' which, though now 'skyed,' hangs in the Louvre. Couture had a great reputation as a teacher and had Manet as one of his pupils. He died at Villiers-le-Bel in 1879.

94. HARLEQUIN AND PIERROT.
    Oil on canvas, $4\frac{3}{4} \times 5\frac{3}{4}$ inches.
Signed with initials: *T. C.*
Coll.: *The Wallace Collection, London.*

REDON, ODILON

1840–1916

Odilon Redon was born in 1840 at Bordeaux, soon after his parents had arrived there from America. Redon senior was a French peasant who had emigrated during the Napoleonic wars and settled in New Orleans, where he had done well for himself. His wife was a Creole. On their return to France the Redons bought an estate in the Landes, where Odilon, who was a delicate boy, spent his childhood and youth. He developed early an interest in botany, literature and philosophy, which he retained all his life. At the age of about twenty he went to Paris to devote himself to art. His first master was Gérôme. Later he studied etching with Rodolphe Bresdin and lithography with Fantin-Latour. His first album of lithographs, 'Dans le Rêve,' appeared in 1879 and was followed by numerous other lithographs published in sets or separately. During the later part of his life he gave up graphic means of expression for oil-paint and pastel. Though he always remained a visionary, he gradually ceased producing imaginary and mystical subjects, mostly inspired by Baudelaire, Poe, Flaubert or Wagner, and took to painting flowers. Redon saw active service during the Franco-Prussian War, was married in 1879 and exhibited at the Salons des Indépendants from their foundation in 1884. He died in Paris in 1916.

99. 'LES YEUX CLOS.'
    Oil on canvas, 15 × 12¼ inches.
Signed: *Odilon Redon*, and dated: *1890*.
Coll.: *Musée du Luxembourg, Paris*.

MONET, CLAUDE-OSCAR

1840–1926

Claude Monet was born in Paris in 1840, and spent his childhood at Le Havre, where his father had a grocery business. When he was fifteen, a local stationer displayed in his shop window some of his caricatures. These

104   SPRING LANDSCAPE

A. Sisley   *The National Gallery, London*

105   FIRST SNOW AT LOUVECIENNES

A. Sisley   *The Lefèvre Galleries, London*

106   A SUMMER AFTERNOON

C. Pissarro

Baron R. von Hirsch

107   THE CRYSTAL PALACE

C. Pissarro

The Lefèvre Galleries, London

attracted the attention of Boudin, who gave him his first lessons in painting. Later Monet went to Paris, where he first studied with Troyon and then with Gleyre, in whose studio he met Cézanne, Renoir, Sisley and Bazille. In 1865 two of his marine pictures were accepted in the Salon. Shortly afterwards he settled in Argenteuil, but during the 1870-71 war he fled abroad, where he encountered the two great influences on the future development of his art: Japanese prints, which he accidentally came across in Holland, and the paintings of Turner, which he saw in London. On his return to France after the war Monet became closely associated with the group of *plein-air* painters who came to be known as the Impressionists. For years he lived in extreme poverty until, in 1883, an exhibition of fifty-six of his paintings, organized by Durand-Ruel, brought in enough money to enable him to buy a small property at Giverny, which remained his home for the rest of his life. From then on Monet's success never abated, his prices rose continually and he became a prosperous man. For the last ten years of his life he was nearly blind, and could distinguish colours only by the way they were placed on the palette. That did not prevent him from working on almost until his death, which occurred at Giverny in 1926, at the age of eighty-six.

100. 'CAMILLE.'

Oil on canvas, $89\frac{1}{2} \times 59\frac{1}{2}$ inches.

'Camille' became in 1870 the artist's first wife. The picture, which is also known as 'La Dame à la Robe Verte,' was exhibited at the Salon of 1866, where it was bought by Arsène Houssaye, the author. It was commented on by Émile Zola, who wrote on the occasion: 'At last in M. Claude Monet we have a man among the usual crowd of eunuchs.'

Signed: *Claude Monet*, and dated: *1866*.
Coll.: *Kunsthalle, Bremen*.

101. ST. GERMAIN L'AUXERROIS.

Oil on canvas, $31 \times 38\frac{1}{2}$ inches.
Signed: *Claude Monet*, and dated: *66*.
Former collection: Faure, Paris.
Coll.: *National Gallerie, Berlin*.

102. THE CANAL AT SAARDAM.

Oil on canvas, $18\frac{3}{4} \times 28\frac{7}{8}$ inches.

Originally bought from the artist by Daubigny in 1870 in London, where they both were then staying.

Formerly in the collection Tavernier, Paris.

Coll.: *Städel'sches Kunstinstitut, Frankfurt.*

SISLEY, ALFRED
1840–1899

Sisley was born in Paris in 1840, of English parents. His father, who was a commission agent, wanted him to go into business, but as it was soon discovered that he showed no aptitude for this, he was allowed to follow his artistic inclinations. In 1862 Sisley entered the studio of Gleyre, where he made friends with Renoir, Monet and Bazille. He then painted in the traditional manner and had pictures accepted at the Salon in 1866 and 1870. It was only after the Franco-Prussian War that he became an Impressionist and took part in the first exhibition of that group in 1874. But even though siding with the artists of the opposition, there was nothing revolutionary in Sisley's nature, and in 1879 he made another, unsuccessful, attempt to enter the official Salon. He was extremely poor; his father had died during the war, ruined, and Sisley never managed to obtain big prices for his pictures. At a sale of his works in 1875, twenty-one canvases fetched only 2455 francs. He lived with his wife and children in the environments of Paris—at Louveciennes, Sèvres, Saint-Cloud and Marly—until, about 1880, he took up residence at Moret-sur-Loing, in the forest of Fontainebleau, where he died in 1899.

103. A VILLAGE BY THE SEINE.

Oil on canvas, $23\frac{1}{8} \times 31\frac{1}{2}$ inches.

Painted in 1872.

Coll.: *Museum of Modern Western Art, Moscow.*

104. SPRING LANDSCAPE.

Oil on canvas, $21\frac{1}{4} \times 28\frac{3}{4}$ inches.

Signed.

Berthe Morisot

108 THE HARBOUR OF LORIENT

Madame Gabriel Thomas

109   THE ARTIST'S FATHER

P. Cézanne

Purchased from the Tooth Galleries and presented to the National Gallery in 1836 through the Roger Fry Memorial Fund.
Coll.: *The National Gallery, London.*

105. FIRST SNOW AT LOUVECIENNES.
  Oil on canvas, $21\frac{1}{4} \times 28\frac{3}{4}$ inches.
  Painted in 1870.
  Signed.
  Formerly in the National Gallerie (*Kronprinz Palais*), Berlin.
  Coll.: *The Lefèvre Galleries, London.*

PISSARRO, CAMILLE-JACOB

1830–1903

Camille Pissarro was born in 1830 at St. Thomas in the Danish West Indies, of a Creole mother and a Jewish father of French nationality. In 1841 his parents sent him to be educated in Paris, but seven years later he was recalled to the West Indies and made to join his father's hardware business. Fritz Melbye, a Dutch artist, then living in the Antilles, gave him his first painting lessons, and in 1855 took him back to Paris. Here he studied in various academies and became a disciple of Corot, whom he greatly admired and whose style he copied until he met some of the Impressionists and associated himself with their movement. At the outbreak of the Franco-Prussian War he fled to London, leaving behind him at Louveciennes some 1500 paintings, which were destroyed by the enemy, who used his house as a butchery. On his return to Paris after the Commune he lived under great financial stress, especially as he was married and had a family to support. He was lucky when he could sell his pictures at prices varying between twenty and fifty francs. Only about 1890 did his work begin to be more appreciated, but at that time his eyes were already giving him great trouble, and when he died in 1903 he was nearly blind.

106. A SUMMER AFTERNOON.
  Oil on canvas, $14\frac{1}{8} \times 20\frac{3}{4}$ inches.
  Painted in 1864.
  Signed.
  Coll.: *Baron Robert von Hirsch, Basle.*

P

107. THE CRYSTAL PALACE.

      Oil on canvas, $15\frac{3}{8} \times 19\frac{3}{4}$ inches.

Painted in 1871.

Signed.

Coll.: *The Lefèvre Galleries, London.*

MORISOT, BERTHE
1841–1895

Berthe Morisot, who was a great-grand-daughter of Fragonard, was born at Bourges in 1841. She first studied painting under Chocarne and Guichard; then, on the suggestion of Corot, under his follower Oudinot. In about 1865 she met Manet, whose great friend she became and whose younger brother, Eugène, she married in 1874. She used to work in Manet's studio and often served him as a model. She is the subject of several of his portraits and also appears in 'Le Balcon' (Luxembourg) and 'Le Repos' (G. Vanderbilt, New York). The influence which Manet exercised upon Berthe Morisot's work gave way after 1885 to that of the Impressionists—Renoir and Monet in particular. She exhibited at the Salon more or less regularly from 1864 till 1873, and from then on at the exhibitions organized by the Impressionists. She held her first personal show in 1892, and died in Paris in 1895.

108. THE HARBOUR OF LORIENT.

      Oil on canvas, $17 \times 28\frac{1}{2}$ inches.

The picture was painted in 1869 and used to belong to Édouard Manet. The figure on the parapet represents Madame Pontillon, a sister of Berthe Morisot.

    Coll.: *Mme. Gabriel Thomas, Meudon, France.*

CÉZANNE, PAUL
1839–1906

Cézanne was born in 1839 at Aix-en-Provence, the son of a wealthy hat-manufacturer who later became a banker. He was educated at the local grammar school and then for a time studied law. In 1863 he decided to follow his real vocation and become a painter. He went to Paris, where he frequented

110   STILL LIFE

P. Cézanne   National Gallery, Oslo

111   THE BLACK MARBLE CLOCK

P. Cézanne   Edward G. Robinson, Esq.

P. Cézanne

112   THE CARD-PLAYERS

The Courtauld Institute of Art, London

113   AFTERNOON IN NAPLES

P. Cézanne

114 GARDANNE

P. Cézanne   *The Barnes Foundation, Philadelphia*

115 LANDSCAPE IN PROVENCE

P. Cézanne   *Captain Victor Cazalet*

various art schools and met Manet, Courbet, Bazille and the Impressionists. In 1867 he married. During the Franco-Prussian War he remained with his family at Aix, and in 1872 returned to Paris, where he stayed till 1877. The rest of his life was spent between the capital and the South of France. He died at Aix in 1906.

Cézanne exhibited but little during his lifetime. He participated at the Impressionist Exhibitions in 1873 and 1877, and had a portrait accepted at the Salon in 1882. In 1899, 1901 and 1902 he was represented at the Salons des Indépendants, and at the Salon d'Automne of 1905 a whole room was devoted to the display of his works. Before 1892, when the dealer Ambroise Vollard began to take an interest in him, the number of pictures he sold was negligible—luckily for him he did not depend on their sales for a living. Even his artist friends, with the exception of Renoir, did not think too highly of his art, and his great influence on the development of modern art only came into being after his death.

3. THE BATHERS.

Oil on canvas, $15\frac{3}{4} \times 21$ inches.
Painted between 1883 and 1887.
A very similar composition is in the collection of Dr. Krebs, Weimar.
Former collections: Dr. Reber, Lausanne; S. Sevadijan, Paris; J. B. Stang, Oslo; Dr. A. Gold, Berlin.
Coll.: *Lord Ivor Spencer-Churchill, London.*

92. 'CÉZANNE CHAUVE.'

Oil on canvas, $13\frac{5}{8} \times 10\frac{1}{2}$ inches.
A self-portrait painted between 1879 and 1882.
Former collections: Bernheim, jeune, Paris; P. M. Turner, London.
Presented to the Gallery by the Trustees of the Courtauld Fund in 1926.
Coll.: *The National Gallery, Millbank, London.*

95. PORTRAIT OF VICTOR CHOQUET.

Oil on canvas, 18×14 inches.
Victor Choquet, a civil servant, was a great friend and admirer of Cézanne. He possessed at least thirty-five of the artist's works.
The picture was painted in 1876-77. When first exhibited at the Impressionists'

Exhibition in Paris in 1877, it was referred to by a critic as '*Billoir au chocolat*'—Billoir being the name of a contemporary murderer.

Signed: *P. Cézanne.*
Compare with Choquet's portrait by Renoir (fig. 96).
Formerly the property of M. Bernheim, jeune, Paris.
Coll.: *Victor Rothschild, Esq., Cambridge.*

109. THE ARTIST'S FATHER.

Oil on canvas, $21\frac{1}{2}\times18$ inches.
Formerly the property of M. Paul Cézanne, fils, Paris.
Coll.: *Maurice Wertheim, Esq., New York.*

110. STILL LIFE.

Oil on canvas, $23\frac{1}{2}\times28\frac{1}{2}$ inches.
Painted about 1889.
Former collections: Auguste Pellerin, Paris; Bernheim, jeune, Paris; acquired by the Oslo Museum in 1910.
Coll.: *National Gallery, Oslo.*

111. THE BLACK MARBLE CLOCK.

Oil on canvas, $21\frac{5}{8}\times29\frac{1}{2}$ inches.
Painted about 1870.
Former collections: Émile Zola, Médan (sold at his sale in 1903); Auguste Pellerin, Paris; Baron Kohner, Budapest; P. Rosenberg, Paris; G. Wildenstein, Paris.
Coll.: *Edward G. Robinson, Esq., Hollywood, U.S.A.*

112. THE CARD-PLAYERS.

Oil on canvas, $23\times27\frac{1}{2}$ inches.
Painted about 1891 in Aix.
A smaller version of the same composition is in the Louvre, and a larger one in the collection of Mr. J. V. Pellerin, Paris. Cézanne also painted two other pictures of the same subject, with four and five figures respectively.
Former collections: Dr. Julius Elias, Berlin; J. B. Stang, Oslo; Dr. Alfred Gold, Berlin.
Coll.: *The Courtauld Institute of Art, London.*

113. AFTERNOON IN NAPLES.

Oil on canvas, $14\frac{1}{2}\times17\frac{5}{8}$ inches.
Painted between 1872 and 1875. There is a water-colour sketch for this picture in the possession of M. Ambroise Vollard.
Coll.: *M. J. V. Pellerin, Paris.*

116 THE THREE BATHERS

P. Cézanne

La Ville de Paris

117 PORTRAIT OF MADAME CÉZANNE

P. Cézanne

S. S. White, Esq.

"MARDI-GRAS"

P. Cézanne

Museum of Modern Western Art, Moscow

119　THE LOVERS

V. Van Gogh

National Gallerie, Berlin

120　THE BRIDGE OF TRINQUETAILLE, ARLES

V. Van Gogh

M. M. Kramarsky

114. GARDANNE.

Oil on canvas, $25\frac{1}{2} \times 39\frac{3}{8}$ inches.

Painted about 1886.

Gardanne is a small town near Aix-en-Provence.

Former collections: A. Vollard, Paris; Egisto Fabbri, Florence; Paul Rosenberg, Paris.

Coll.: *The Barnes Foundation, Philadelphia.*

115. LANDSCAPE IN PROVENCE. (*Le Village sur la Hauteur.*)

Oil on canvas, 55×67 inches.

Painted between 1882 and 1885.

Former collections: A. Vollard, Paris; A. Flechtheim, Berlin; Count Kessler, Weimar; Marquis de Brion, Paris.

Coll.: *Captain Victor Cazalet, M.C., M.P., London.*

116. THE THREE BATHERS.

Oil on canvas, $19\frac{5}{8} \times 19\frac{5}{8}$ inches.

Painted between 1879 and 1882.

Formerly the property of M. Henri Matisse, Nice, who presented it to the city of Paris.

Coll.: *La Ville de Paris.*

117. PORTRAIT OF MME. CÉZANNE.

Oil on canvas, $18 \times 14\frac{7}{8}$ inches.

Painted about 1885.

Former collections: Henri Matisse, Nice; Paul Rosenberg, Paris; Reid and Lefèvre, London.

Coll.: *S. S. White, Esq., Ardmore, U.S.A.*

118. 'MARDI-GRAS.'

Oil on canvas, $40 \times 31\frac{3}{4}$ inches.

Painted in Paris in 1888.

Cézanne's son, Paul, posed for the figure of the Harlequin, and M. Louis Guillaume for that of the Pierrot. Three oil studies of the Harlequin are in existence, one of which now belongs to Mr. Victor Rothschild, Cambridge.

Former collections: V. Choquet, Paris; Durand-Ruel, Paris; Stchoukine, Moscow.

Coll.: *Museum of Modern Western Art, Moscow.*

Q

VAN GOGH, VINCENT-WILLEM
1853–1890

Vincent Van Gogh, born in 1853 at Groot-Zundert, Holland, was the son of a clergyman. He had a turbulent and passionate nature, which, coupled with ill-health and poverty, eventually led him into the mad-house and to a violent end. In his youth Van Gogh was employed by a firm of picture-dealers, but, as a result of an unreciprocated love affair, he left his job and took to preaching. As an evangelist preacher he was sent in 1878 to the mining district of the Borinage in Belgium, but was soon dismissed for unconventional zest. In 1880 he decided to devote himself to painting and worked for a time with his brother-in-law, Anton Mauve, at The Hague, where, spending all his meagre resources on buying paint, he nearly starved. During his stay in Holland he had other sentimental misadventures: he fell in love with a widowed cousin who did not like him; lived with a prostitute, whom he wanted but failed to reform, and had an abortive romance with a woman who committed suicide.

In 1886 Van Gogh went to live with his younger brother Theo in Paris, where contact with Pissarro, Seurat, Lautrec, Degas, Gauguin and Bernard, with whom he spent a summer at Asnières, greatly stimulated his art. He painted portraits which he sold at 20 francs, and exhibited his pictures in the shop of Tanguy, the colour merchant. In 1888, his health becoming worse, he moved to Arles, where he was later joined by Gauguin. Towards the close of the same year occurred his first fits of madness. In one fit he flung a glass at the head of Gauguin, causing his departure, and in another cut off his ear, which he sent as a Christmas present to a girl he had met in a café. He was made to enter Arles Hospital, and later sent to the Asylum at St. Rémy. During his periods of sanity, he worked with feverish impetuosity and produced some of his finest paintings. In May 1890 he was placed under the care of Dr. Gachet at Auvers-sur-Oise, near Paris, where, two months after his arrival, in a moment of acute depression, he shot himself.

Theo Van Gogh, Vincent's correspondence with whom constitutes a precious autobiography, died of grief and worry half a year later and was buried at Auvers beside his brother.

119. THE LOVERS.

Oil on canvas, $29\frac{1}{2} \times 36\frac{1}{4}$ inches.

Painted in Arles in October 1888.

Described by Van Gogh in *Letters to his Brother*—letter 556 (with sketch), where he states that this picture 'makes the fourth canvas of "The Poet's Garden," which is the scheme of decoration for Gauguin's room.'

Former collections: Uttwil, Amsterdam; Carl Sternheim, Munich.

Coll.: *National Gallerie, Berlin.*

120. THE BRIDGE OF TRINQUETAILLE, ARLES.

Oil on canvas, $29 \times 36\frac{1}{2}$ inches.

Painted in Arles in October 1888.

Described by Van Gogh in *Letters to his Brother*—letter 552 (with sketch).

Former collections: Mme. J. Van Gogh-Bonger, Amsterdam; A. W. von Heymel, Berlin; H. von Tschudi, Munich; Silberberg, Breslau.

Coll.: *M. M. Kramarsky, Amsterdam.*

121. THE POSTMAN ROULIN.

Oil on canvas, $31\frac{1}{2} \times 25$ inches.

There are numerous references to Roulin in the artist's *Letters to his Brother*. In one of them (letter 516) Roulin is described as 'a big bearded face, very like Socrates. A violent Republican like Tanguy. A man more interesting than most.'

Painted in Arles in 1888. There exist five other portraits of the same model.

Former collections: C. Hoogendijk, The Hague; Uttwil, Amsterdam; Carl Sternheim, Munich.

Coll.: *Robert Treat Paine, Esq., Boston, U.S.A.*

122. PORTRAIT OF THE HEAD WARDER OF THE ASYLUM.

Oil on canvas, $24\frac{1}{4} \times 18\frac{1}{4}$ inches.

Painted in the hospital at St. Rémy in September 1889.

Referred to by Van Gogh in *Letters to his Brother*—letters 604 and 605.

He says of the warder: 'He was at the hospital at Marseilles through two periods of cholera, altogether he is a man who has seen an enormous lot of suffering and death, and in his face there is a sort of contemplative calm, so that the face of Guizot—for there is something of that in this head but different—comes involuntarily to my memory. But he is of the people and simpler.'

Remained in the artist's family till 1908.

Coll.: *Mme. G. Dübi-Müller, Solothurn, Switzerland.*

123. STILL LIFE.

Oil on canvas, $25\frac{3}{4} \times 32$ inches.

Painted in 1888.

Described by Van Gogh in *Letters to his Brother*—letter 489 (with sketch).

Signed: *Vincent*.

Former collections: Mme. J. Van Gogh-Bonger, Amsterdam; Uttwil, Amsterdam.

Coll.: *Mme. Carl Sternheim, Paris*.

124. 'L'ARLÉSIENNE.'

Oil on canvas, $36\frac{3}{4} \times 29\frac{1}{4}$ inches.

Portrait of Mme. Ginoux painted in Arles in November 1888.

Referred to by Van Gogh in *Letters to his Brother*—letters 559 and 573. According to these the picture was painted in one hour's time. Another version of the picture, in which the umbrella and gloves are replaced by two books, is in the A. Lewisohn collection, New York.

Former collections: Mme. J. Van Gogh-Bonger, Amsterdam; Carl Sternheim, Munich; Frau von Friedlander-Fould, Berlin.

Coll.: *Baronne Goldschmidt-Rothschild*.

125. THE ARTIST'S BEDROOM AT ARLES.

Oil on canvas, $28\frac{5}{8} \times 36\frac{1}{2}$ inches.

Mentioned in *Letters to his Brother*—letters 554 (with sketch) and 555. In letter 573 Van Gogh says: 'When I saw my canvases again after my illness the one that seemed the best to me was the bedroom.'

There exist two other versions of the same subject with slight variations.

Painted in October 1888.

Coll.: *V. W. Van Gogh, Amsterdam*.

GAUGUIN, PAUL

1848–1903

Gauguin was born in Paris in 1848 and was on his mother's side of Spanish descent. His father was a French journalist who in 1851 emigrated with his family to Peru, where young Paul remained till 1858, when he was sent back to France to be educated in a Jesuit seminary at Orléans. From the age of seventeen to twenty-three he served in the mercantile marine. Then he joined a firm of Paris stockbrokers, and in 1873 married a young Danish woman by whom he had five children. For ten years he led the

121   THE POSTMAN ROULIN

V. Van Gogh

Robert Treat Paine, Esq.

122   PORTRAIT OF THE HEAD WARDER OF THE ASYLUM

V. Van Gogh

Madame G. Dübi-Müller

123   STILL LIFE

V. Van Gogh   *Madame Carl Sternheim*

124   "L'ARLÉSIENNE"

V. Van Gogh

Baronne Goldschmidt-Rothschild

125   THE ARTIST'S BEDROOM AT ARLES

comfortable existence of a well-to-do *bourgeois*, but in 1883 he suddenly gave up his job so as to be able to devote all his time to painting, which till then he had practised only as a hobby. He soon found himself without means; his wife left him to rejoin her family in Denmark whilst he found temporary employment as a bill-poster. In 1886 he exhibited some pictures at the last Impressionist Exhibition in the rue Laffitte and spent the summer in Brittany, where he met Van Gogh. In 1887 he travelled out to Martinique, but fell ill there and had to come home. The following years he spent between Paris and Brittany. He also went to Arles to join Van Gogh, but the visit was cut short owing to the latter's fits of violence. In 1891 Gauguin managed to make about 10,000 francs by the sale of thirty of his canvases and departed for Tahiti, where he spent two years. The death of an uncle, who left him a small legacy, brought him back to France. He held an exhibition at the Durand-Ruel galleries, which was a great *succès d'estime*, but brought in little money. Disheartened, tired of civilization, the victim of a venereal disease, in 1895 he again set forth for the Pacific Islands. He lived in Tahiti till 1901, then went to the Marquesas Isles, where he died in 1903.

126. 'ARII MATAMOE.'
> Oil on canvas, $17\frac{3}{4} \times 29\frac{1}{4}$ inches.

Painted in Tahiti in 1892. The picture represents a 'wake' by the severed head of a dead chief.

Gauguin gave the following description of the picture: 'Une tête de canaque bien arrangée sur un coussin blanc dans un palais de mon invention et gardée par les femmes de mon invention aussi.'

Bought at the Gauguin sale in 1895 for 400 francs.
Coll.: *M. Guillaume Lerolle, Paris.*

127. RIDERS BY THE SEA.
> Oil on canvas, $28\frac{1}{4} \times 36\frac{1}{8}$ inches.

Signed: *Paul Gauguin*, and dated: *1902*.
Coll.: *The Wallraf-Richartz Museum, Cologne.*

128. AN INTERIOR IN TAHITI.
> Oil on canvas, $28\frac{3}{4} \times 36\frac{1}{4}$ inches.

Signed: *P. Gauguin*, and dated: *91*.
Coll.: *Mme. Georges Menier, Paris.*

R

129. THE THREE DOGS.

      Oil on canvas, 36×25 inches.

Signed: *P. Go*, and dated: *88*.

From the collection of M. Ambroise Vollard.

Coll.: *Mme. Carl Sternheim, Paris.*

SEURAT, GEORGES-PIERRE
1859–1891

Georges Seurat was born in Paris in 1859. His academic training under Lehmann at the École des Beaux-Arts had no bearings on the consequent development of his art. He became interested in the discoveries made by Helmholtz, Rood, Chevreul and other scientists about the phenomena of the spectrum. Basing himself on their theories, he evolved a scientific method of painting founded on the principle of the optical blending of pure colours applied separately on to the canvas and not previously mixed on the palette. He thus originated 'divisionism,' or, as he preferred to call it, 'chromo-luminism,' and soon collected around him some followers—Signac, Luce, Cross and others, who called themselves Neo-Impressionists and exhibited for the first time as a group at a gallery in the rue Laffitte in 1886. There Seurat's 'Dimanche à la Grande Jatte' (Chicago Museum) caused a scandal. Seurat was a regular exhibitor at the Salons des Indépendants from their foundation in 1884 until his death, which occurred in Paris in 1891.

2. LE BEC DU HOC, GRANDCAMP.

      Oil on canvas, 25½×31½ inches.

Painted in 1885, and first exhibited in 1887 at the 'Société des Vingt' in Brussels, where it was bought by H. Van Cutsem for 300 francs. During his lifetime Seurat sold only one other picture—'Le Chahut,' which was acquired by his friend Gustave Kahn in 1890.

Former collections: M. Van Cutsem, Brussels; M. Kocherthaler, Madrid.

Coll.: *Kenneth Clark, Esq., London.*

130. THE PEASANTS. (*Les Terrassiers.*)

      Oil on panel, 6×10 inches.

A sketch painted about 1883.

Coll.: *Captain Victor Cazalet, M.C., M.P., London.*

P. Gauguin   126   "ARII MATAMOE"    A. G. Lerolle

130   THE PEASANTS

G. Seurat   *Captain Victor Cazalet*

131   BOY IN A FIELD

G. Seurat   *Private Collection, Scotland*

131. BOY IN A FIELD.

Oil on canvas, 25×31¾ inches.

Painted in 1883.

Formerly owned by private collectors in Berlin and New York and by the Lefèvre Galleries, London.

Coll.: *Private ownership, Scotland.*

132. THE MODEL: FRONT VIEW.

Oil on panel, 9¾×6¼ inches.

One of the studies done in 1887 for the large composition '*Les Poseuses*,' now in the Barnes collection, Philadelphia, which it took the artist a year to paint. In a letter addressed to Octave Mans, President of the 'Société des Vingt,' in 1889, Seurat wrote: 'As for my *Poseuses*, I have some difficulty in fixing the price. I reckon as my expenses one year at seven francs a day: you see where that leads us. In short, all I can say is that the personality of the buyer may compensate me for the difference between his price and mine.' The picture then remained unsold. The present study was first exhibited in 1887 at the Third Exhibition of the Société des Artistes Indépendants in Paris.

Coll.: *M. Félix Fénéon, Paris.*

133. 'LA POUDREUSE.'

Oil on canvas, 37½×31¼ inches.

Painted in 1890, and exhibited the same year at the Salon des Indépendants.

Former collections: Félix Fénéon, Paris; Kelekian, Paris; John Quinn, New York.

Coll.: *The Courtauld Institute of Art, London.*

134. THE BANKS OF THE SEINE. (*Île de la Grande Jatte.*)

Oil on canvas, 25⅝×32 inches.

Painted about 1887.

The Île de la Grande Jatte, near Paris, supplied Seurat with themes for many pictures, including the large 'Dimanche à la Grande Jatte' now in the Chicago Museum.

Presented to the Brussels Museum by Mlle. Anna Boch.

Coll.: *Musée de l'Art Moderne, Brussels.*

135. LA BAIGNADE.

Oil on canvas, 71¾×144¼ inches.

Painted in 1883-84. Exhibited at the first Salon des Indépendants held in the courtyard of the Tuileries.

Signed: *Seurat.*

Formerly in the possession of M. Félix Fénéon, Paris.

Presented to the Gallery by the Trustees of the Courtauld Fund in 1924.

Coll.: *The National Gallery, Millbank, London.*

136. 'LA PARADE.'

   Oil on canvas, 39½×59 inches.
Painted in 1887-88.
First exhibited, together with 'Les Poseuses,' at the Salon des Indépendants in 1888. Formerly in the collection of M. Félix Fénéon, Paris.
Coll.: *Roland F. Knoedler, Esq., New York.*

137. THE HARBOUR OF GRAVELINES.

   Oil on canvas, 26½×31½ inches.
Painted in 1890.
Former collections: Félix Fénéon, Paris; Alfred Flechtheim, Berlin.
Coll.: *M. Rolf de Maré, Paris,*

138. THE ENTRANCE TO HONFLEUR HARBOUR.

   Oil on canvas, 21×25⅛ inches.
Painted in 1886.
Signed: *Seurat.*
Former collections: Folkwang Museum, Hagen, Westphalia; Alfred Flechtheim, Berlin; Rolf de Maré, Paris.
Coll.: *The Barnes Foundation, Philadelphia, U.S.A.*

ROUSSEAU, HENRI, CALLED LE DOUANIER
1844–1910

Henri Rousseau, known as 'Le Douanier,' was the son of an iron-monger and was born at Laval (Mayenne) in 1844. He took part in the Mexican War (1862–67) as a regimental musician, and in the Franco-Prussian War as a Sergeant. He was later employed by the Paris *Octroi*, and was twice married, surviving both his wives. He probably first began painting about 1884. His works always remained primitive in conception and naïve in execution, but their gentle sensitiveness eventually even opened for him the doors of the Louvre, where his 'La Charmeuse de Serpents' now hangs. Except in 1899 and 1900 Rousseau was a regular exhibitor at the Salons des Indépendants from 1886 until 1910, and also had his pictures accepted at the Salon d'Automne in 1905, 1906 and 1907. Though he had genuine admirers in such people as Alfred Jarry, the author of *Ubu-Roi*, the poet Guillaume

133 "LA POUDREUSE" G. Seurat

The Courtauld Institute of Art, London

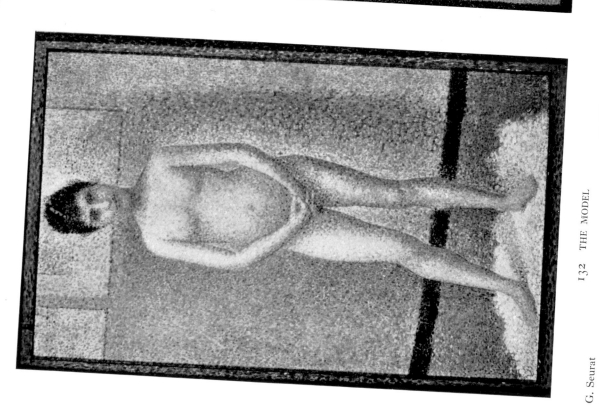

G. Seurat

132 THE MODEL

M. Félix Fénéon

Apollinaire, the painter Robert Delaunay and the German art-critic Wilhelm Uhde, he found few purchasers for his pictures and gave most of them away to his friends or in exchange for the necessities of life. He died in Paris in 1910.

139. THE SLEEPING GYPSY.

Oil on canvas.
Painted in 1897. Exhibited the same year at the Salon des Indépendants.
Signed.
Former collection: John Quinn, New York.
Coll.: *Private Collection, Switzerland.*

140. 'L'OCTROI.'

Oil on canvas, $14\frac{1}{2} \times 12\frac{1}{4}$ inches.
Signed.
Former collection: Alfred Flechtheim, Berlin.
Coll.: *Samuel Courtauld, Esq., London.*

141. SELF-PORTRAIT.

Oil on canvas, $57\frac{1}{2} \times 44\frac{3}{4}$ inches.
On the palette which Rousseau is holding are inscribed the names of his two wives: 'Clémence et Joséphine.' The landscape is meant to represent the quays in Paris opposite the Louvre.
Signed: *Henri Rousseau.*
Coll.: *Gallery of Modern Art, Prague.*

S

136 "LA PARADE"

G. Seurat

137   THE HARBOUR, GRAVELINES

G. Seurat

M. Rolf de Maré

138   THE ENTRANCE TO HONFLEUR HARBOUR

G. Seurat

The Barnes Foundation, Philadelphia

139   THE SLEEPING GIPSY

Henri Rousseau   *Private Collection, Switzerland*

140   "L'OCTROI"

Henri Rousseau   *Samuel Courtauld, Esq.*

141   SELF-PORTRAIT

Henri Rousseau

Gallery of Modern Art, Prague

POSTSCRIPT
By ALFRED FLECHTHEIM

I

IN October 1936, I, with a group of English and French friends—the painter Paul Maze, the collectors Lord Ivor Churchill and the Earl of Sandwich, and the art-dealer Paul Rosenberg—had the pleasure of selecting and hanging the 125 pictures which formed the Exhibition of French Nineteenth-Century Painting, organized by the Anglo-French Art and Travel Society at the New Burlington Galleries, London. It was an exhibition that caused an immediate stir, and remained, for the month of its duration, the Mecca of art-lovers from all over the British Isles, and, in fact, from all over the world.

But a certain number of visitors and critics asked the inevitable question: 'Why *French* art? Why French art again and again? Why not the art of other countries? English art, for instance, especially as France does not seem to show the same interest in it as England has always shown in the art of France.'

I had heard these questions asked again and again while still a dealer in Germany, where I had arranged shows of a similar kind. And I know that organizers of exhibitions in the United States, the Netherlands, Sweden, Switzerland and elsewhere have been asked them too.

The answer is, I suppose, that each country has at different periods its particular genius in artistic production. England, for instance, has her incomparable poetry. 'English poetry is the greatest in the world, and the painters must pay for it,' Clive Bell has said; but it must not be forgotten that English poetry and literature exercised a strong influence on the Romanticism of Delacroix and his followers. Shakespeare alone provided the inspiration for that artist's 'Hamlet and Horatio,' 'Ophelia's Death' and 'Hamlet on the Corpse of Polonius,' for Chassériau's 'Le Coucher de Desdémone,' and Corot's 'Macbeth and the Three Witches.' Scott (*Kenilworth* and *Ivanhoe*) and Byron (*The Prisoner of Chillon, Marino Faliero*) exerted a similar influence. Later in the century the works of Dickens were to inspire that excellent draughtsman, Gustave Doré, to produce his 'Misères de Londres' and 'Les Marchandes de Fleurs,' while *Alice in Wonderland* seems in part responsible for the youngest artistic movement of our own times, Surréalisme.

T

English painting reached its zenith during the eighteenth and early nineteenth centuries. Works by English portraitists and landscape painters of that period are displayed in the best public and private galleries all over the world. In 1924, just a hundred years after the first exhibition in Paris of Constable's 'The Hay Wain,' which made such a great impression on Delacroix, E. V. Lucas wrote in *The Times* about the Louvre: 'The two English Cabinets here claim attention. The Louvre has not many English pictures, but they are good and of impressive seriousness. But it is perhaps Constable and Bonington, Turner and Wilson that give the little collection its greatest value. One of the Constables, a cottage, seems to have all Rousseau in it.'

Turner, Bonington and Constable seem, indeed, to have had during the nineteenth century a far stronger influence on the painting of France than on that of England. In England their influence was lost in the literary ebullience of Pre-Raphaelitism. But the artists of the Barbizon School, and the Impressionists who followed them, were to understand the message of these painters. Though every great art movement since the Empire has had France as its background—classicism, romanticism, naturalism, realism, impressionism, post-impressionism, fauvism, cubism—it cannot be denied that English landscape painting during the early nineteenth century accomplished a great pioneer work. Surréalisme—if one excludes Pre-Raphaelitism, which was English and national in character, and, incidentally, wholly subversive to the influence of Constable and Turner—is the first artistic movement of modern times which has not a wholly French flavour. Fuseli and Blake, the Italian Giorgio de Chirico and the German-Swiss Paul Klee were its true creators.

Apart from this single manifestation, the best artists of all countries have walked in the footsteps of the French masters. In England all of them, to quote Clive Bell, 'except Sickert, who descends from Degas, and Steer, who descends from the Impressionists, and through the Impressionists from the French eighteenth century, are children or grandchildren of Cézanne.' In Germany there were Liebermann and Leibl; of the latter, Douglas Cooper has written, in his preface to the catalogue of a recent Courbet Exhibition in London: 'In 1869 Courbet visited Munich for an International Exhibition when some of his pictures were on view. He was warmly received into the côterie of Leibl, whom he had previously met in Paris, and it was at his instigation that Courbet was decorated by Ludwig II, friend and patron of Wagner. All the artists of Munich were very eager to watch him at work; and so it was that one day in Kaulbach's studio, taking the red-haired servant girl for a model, he produced for their interest the picture "La Femme de Munich," which now, alas, has disappeared.' In Belgium there is James Ensor, in Norway Edward Munch. The Dutchmen Jongkind and Van Gogh; the Englishman Sisley; Pissarro, who originally came from the Danish West Indies; the Spaniards Picasso and Juan Gris, all became masters in France and turned their backs on their own countries.

II

It was probably in the rue la Boétie in Paris that the term *Le Grand Siècle* was first coined to describe the French art of the nineteenth century. Today there is no serious critic, artist or art historian who would protest against its use. 'From the neo-classicism of David to the Fauves, what an extraordinary range of painters of absolutely first rank make their appearance, what a variety and what a wealth of talent,' Alfred Leroy has written, with the pardonable pride of a Frenchman, in his very instructive *Histoire de la Peinture Française*. 'This century, once lightly dismissed as "ridiculous," now on the contrary shows itself by far the most representative in the great florescence of plastic art, as, indeed, in the fecundity and intensity of its intellectual life.' But this florescence did not cease with the Fauves and Matisse, for they in their turn were followed by the Cubists and Picasso, coming, as it were, as the fulfilment of the dreams and efforts of Cézanne, that tragic genius who, like Moses on Mount Horeb, was to look over the promised land but never to enter it. 'I carry on obstinately,' he wrote to Vollard in 1903, 'I catch glimpses of the promised land. Shall I be as the great leader of the Hebrews, or shall I enter upon it one day?'

During the last thirty years or so, a fine representative collection of French nineteenth-century painting has consistently attracted at least as much interest as similar collections of Italian Primitives, old Dutch or eighteenth-century masters. The room in the London National Gallery in which are hung the works of Ingres, Delacroix, Manet, Cézanne and Renoir, offers today as intense an artistic experience as the Sienese or Flemish rooms, the Titians, the Rembrandts or the Spanish painters.

In Germany, the victory of the French nineteenth century was fought and won in 1911. Hugo von Tschudi, that great art-lover and connoisseur, had, as Director of the Bavarian Royal collections, invited the Hungarian collector, Marcell von Nemes, to exhibit his collection in the Munich Pinakothek — his Primitives, his fifteen Grecos, his Titians, Tintorettos, Rembrandts, Hals, Goyas, Delacroixs, Courbets, Manets, Renoirs, Van Goghs and his ten Cézannes. Many critics of the older school protested at what they termed 'a sacrilegious mixture.' Wilhelm von Bode, Germany's art dictator and the creator of the Kaiser Friedrich Museum in Berlin, was particularly emphatic on the subject. He was a friend of the Kaiser, and he hated Greco! When the Mendelssohn family offered the 'Laocoon,' which now belongs to Prince Paul of Yugoslavia, as a gift to his Museum, Bode refused it. Von Bode disliked Tschudi, whom the Kaiser had driven from the National Gallery in Berlin for having accepted the gift of a fine collection of French pictures without his permission. But Prince Rupprecht of Bavaria, in the face of the opposition of the Kaiser, of his grandfather, the Prince Regent, and of all the Munich painters, succeeded in securing Tschudi for Munich. A result of Tschudi's appointment as director was the Nemes Exhibition and the formation in a German public gallery of a collection of French nineteenth-century pictures—pictures which were offered, mostly by Prussian art-lovers, directly in opposition to the wishes of the Kaiser and von Bode, as a personal tribute to Hugo von Tschudi.

The Nemes Exhibition marked the triumph of French nineteenth-century art in Germany, and revealed to the public that these pictures were of a stature comparable only with those of the greatest masters of the past. No one nowadays would dream of protesting against the hanging of the 'Bar des Folies Bergère,' the 'Parapluies' or the 'Montagne St. Victoire' near to Piero's 'Nativity,' Titian's 'Vendramin Family' or Rembrandt's self-portraits, while men like Bode, despite their definite merits and knowledge, today seem old-fashioned to say the least of it. Incidentally, the only collection in Europe today that reminds me of Nemes is that of Reinhart, where you can find Cranachs and Grecos, Renoirs and Cézannes, side by side.

POSTSCRIPT

Among the first foreign collectors of French art was Frederick II, Prussia's greatest king, who acquired pictures by contemporary French painters—Boucher, Chardin, Fragonard, Watteau—whilst his armies were defeating the French on the battlefields of Silesia.

One of the first and most influential English purchasers of French nineteenth-century pictures was the Marquess of Hertford. To his world-famous old masters, his matchless *dixhuitièmes* and his wonderful series of Boningtons he added one picture by Corot, twenty-eight by Decamps, two by Delacroix, twelve by Delaroche, six by Prud'hon, twenty-two by Horace Vernet, two by Géricault and sixteen by Meissonier. But, as Bernard Falk wrote in *Old Q's Daughter*, 'as a collector Lord Hertford is possibly not to be compared with a man like Sir Hugh Lane, who, as shown by his Monet, Manet, Renoir, Corot, Daumier, Pissarro and Cézanne purchases, managed to spot many of the great artists of the last century before their work was world-famous. The Marquess, great as are his claims to the art-lover's gratitude, made no sensational discoveries and challenged no settled theories.' With Lane it was a different matter. But, when his wonderful collection was hanging in the small dark Municipal Art Gallery of Dublin, where the titles and artists' names were only written in Irish, no one came to see it.

Frank Rutter has referred to exhibitions of French painting in London in his amusing *critique* of the 1936 show, *Revenons à nos Moutons*. 'Nor are the examples of French Impressionists here shown,' he wrote, 'comparable to the wealth of masterpieces included in the Durand-Ruel Exhibition at the Grafton Galleries in 1905. A proof of this is the way in which Renoir's "Dancing in the Country" stands out in the present exhibition, whereas for all its brilliance it was but one of a dozen in the 1905 exhibition, and was itself eclipsed by the same master's still more exquisite "Young Girls at the Piano." Even Cézanne and Gauguin were more richly represented in Roger Fry's 1910 Post-Impressionist Exhibition.' Rutter perhaps forgets that in 1905 and 1910 many of the most enthusiastic visitors to the 1936 exhibition were still in their swaddling clothes or else unborn. He continues: 'The time to say this was in 1905, when there were practically no paintings by Degas, Manet, Pissarro, etc.; when they were considered unacceptable by the Trustees [of the National Gallery] even as a free gift; when there

105

was not even an example of Boudin at Trafalgar Square till I was able to purchase one with the aid of subscriptions from readers of the *Sunday Times* and present it in 1906, through the National Art Collections Fund.' But London quickly remedied its deficiency. To add to the Lane pictures came the splendid treasures resulting from the enthusiasm of Mr. and Mrs. Courtauld, the fine pictures lent to the Tate Gallery by Sir William Burrell and the acquisitions of the National Art Collections Fund, which secured for the London Galleries works by Corot, Courbet, Daumier, Degas, Seurat and other artists; to say nothing of the bequest of the Ionides collection to the Victoria and Albert Museum, which contains one of the most beautiful Degas.

Long before this period New York had its important nineteenth-century pictures, bought for the Havemeyers and other American families by Mary Cassat, the painter; while in Philadelphia Dr. Barnes had already laid the foundations of his magnificent collection. In Russia, Morosoff and Stchukin had begun the collections that now hang upon the walls of the Museum of Western Art in Moscow, while Germany, as we have already seen, had her von Tschudi.

Since then innumerable books and articles have been written on the nineteenth-century painters. *Catalogues raisonnés* have been published on Ingres, Delacroix, Corot, Manet, Daumier, Van Gogh, Lautrec and Cézanne; Félix Fénéon is preparing one on Seurat. The works of Renoir found in his studio at Cagnes after his death have been catalogued and reproduced in two volumes. Some of these books are, perhaps, on the fulsome side, but together they go to show the intense interest in this period, shared by specialists and amateurs alike.

The achievements of the French nineteenth-century painters have been recorded by art historians, poets, critics, dealers and by the artists themselves. The best of the earlier books on the Impressionists was written by one of their personal friends, Théodore Duret, who published in 1878 *Les Peintres Impressionnistes*. This was a mere brochure of thirty-five pages. In 1885 followed the same writer's *Critique d'Avant Garde*, a volume of fifty pages. In 1883 J-K. Huysmans published his *L'Art Moderne*, and in 1886 Félix Fénéon his *Impressionnistes*, in connection with the symbolist review *Vogue*. Émile Verhaeren wrote on the new painting in the *Journal de Bruxelles* in 1890, and von Tschudi in the same year in *Die Kunst für Alle*. In 1893 George Moore brought out his *Modern Painting*, and in 1906, in Dublin, his *Reminiscences of Impressionist Painting*. Frederic Wedmore wrote an article on the Impressionists in *The Fortnightly Review* as early as January 1883, on the occasion of the exhibition at Dowdeswell and Dowdeswell's gallery at 133 New Bond Street. In the United States in 1892 C. Waern wrote on them in *The Atlantic Review*, and Browner in *The Scribblers' Magazine*. Books are available in English by Dr. Barnes, Roger Fry, Clive Bell, Thomas Craven, Wynford Dewhurst, Jan and Cora Gordon, G. Mourey, R. H. Wilenski and other writers. But the book which has had, perhaps, the greatest significance of all is Meier-Graefe's *Entwicklungs-geschichte der modernen Malerei*, which appeared about 1900 and was trans-lated into many languages. Leo von König, the painter and Meier-Graefe's friend, wrote in his obituary of the critic in *Die Neue Rundschau* in 1935: 'It was as if the spring wind had flung the windows open and fresh air had penetrated the musty studios. This book was an achievement full of new starting points for future art historians. The first to realize this were we artists for whom it was a vital experience. Facts were expressed in it which until then we had but vaguely perceived in our subconscious mind. Today, since one art tendency has followed another in rapid succession, this has been forgotten. Meier-Graefe might have written more mature and better books than this *Entwicklungsgeschichte*—later he himself became over-involved—but never again has a book of his been more stimulating.'

Meier-Graefe, incidentally, had been the leading spirit in the movement inaugurated in 1898 by Bing, the famous dealer in Japanese works of art, when he moved his *objets d'art* to the second floor of his gallery in the rue de Provence and entirely changed the character of the rest. 'L'Art Nouveau,' it was significantly rechristened. The façade was designed by Frank Brangwyn, and the contents were international to say the least of it. There were terra-cottas and wool embroideries by Maillol, Neo-Gothic marbles by the Belgian Minne, pictures and decorative work, including screens, chintzes, carpets, wallpapers, tapestries and furnishing materials by Seurat,[1] Signac, Cross, Bonnard, Vuillard, Sickert, Maurice Denis and others. There were books and drawings by Beardsley and Gordon Craig, vases from Nancy by Émile

---

[1] His ' Le Chahut ' was sold there for 900 francs, and sketches painted on the lids of cigar boxes fetched less than 100 francs apiece.

107

Gallé, glasswork by Lalique, cartoons by Lautrec, which Tiffany of New York executed in coloured glass, and furnishings by Henry van de Velde. This excellent Belgian architect and decorator had started as a Neo-Impressionist painter; now he was attempting to modernize the abstract ornament of William Morris. One of the achievements of 'Art Nouveau' was to draw attention once again to the innovations of the great English creator, writer and Socialist.

Europe welcomed the venture with enthusiasm. In Glasgow, Mackintosh carried the torch into Cranston's Teashop and the New School of Art. In Brussels, the Viennese architect, Hoffmann, built a striking new house for M. Stoclet, the collector of primitive art. In Munich there were the 'Jugend' Restaurant and the 'Jugend' Review—the Germans called this Art Nouveau 'Jugendstil.' Klimt in Vienna, Axel Gallen in Finland, Toorop and Thorn Trikker in Holland, in Norway Edward Munch, who combined a Gauguin-esque style with Nordic mysticism—all responded to the new influence. Only the French remained sceptical. They did not like Bing's shop, or what it represented—'yachting style,' Edmond de Goncourt dubbed it super-ciliously. They still preferred to hang even their Impressionist pictures in Louis XV and Louis XVI Salons. But the rue Laffitte, where most of the dealers in the new painters had their galleries, still had to fight for them, though at Vollard's advanced connoisseurs were already beginning to ask for Cézannes. The famous collector Moreau-Nelaton declared that 'Art Nouveau' was not in keeping with French taste, that only foreigners could create anything so un-French as this gallery. The shop failed; Bing returned to Japan and Meier-Graefe to Germany. But he soon returned to Paris to busy himself with the writing of his *Entwicklungsgeschichte*.

Other works followed on Cézanne, Corot, Courbet, Daumier, Degas, Delacroix, Gauguin, Manet, Renoir and Van Gogh, and writers in every country began to imitate the achievement of the great German critic. Now there is no artist of this period who has not his more or less able historian. Ambroise Vollard, that great *marchand de tableaux créateur*, published his recollections on Degas, Renoir and Cézanne, and his experiences as a dealer, which are a mine of information. In the already referred to catalogue of the Courbet Exhibition at the Mayor Gallery no fewer than nineteen mono-graphs on that painter are enumerated, while Lionello Venturi, in his admirable *catalogue raisonné* of the works of Cézanne, published by Paul Rosenberg in 1936, cites the astonishing number of 561 books and articles devoted to that master. Certainly one of the best is Roger Fry's monograph. Books of this kind, both by professional critics and amateurs, continue to appear in every language, and have even found their way into Yiddish and Japanese. They vary from pocket volumes published at a shilling to sumptuous *éditions de luxe* running into many guineas.

Strange is the fate of Seurat. Only two or three books have been published on this painter, and Vollard, in his reminiscences, only mentions him once, and then but briefly, giving far greater prominence to such men as de Groux and Luce. If the American lawyer-collector, John Quinn, had not bequeathed one of his masterpieces, 'Le Cirque,' to the Louvre, one of France's greatest geniuses would remain entirely unrepresented in his own country. During his lifetime Seurat only sold two pictures. They were 'Le Bec de Hoc à Grandcamp' (which now belongs to Mr. Kenneth Clark) for 300 francs to H. von Cutsem, and 'Le Chahut,' which was purchased by his friend, the poet Gustave Kahn. Kahn sold it later to Meier-Graefe, and it now hangs in the Kröller collection at The Hague. It is an interesting commentary that galleries now owning works by Seurat include the Louvre, the National Gallery, the Museums of Brussels and Prague, the Art Institute of Chicago, the Barnes Foundation and the Museum of Western Art in Moscow.

In 1900 Fénéon organized a Seurat Exhibition, including all his most important works, at the offices of *La Révue Blanche*. The prices were still very low. The only sales were 'La Parade' and 'La Rade de Grandcamp,' which went to MM. Josse and Gaston Bernheim, the only dealers then bold enough to buy a Seurat, for a few hundred francs apiece. T. W. Earp wrote on the occasion of the Seurat Exhibition held at Wildenstein's in London in 1937: 'A conservative estimate of the value of his pictures there would be £100,000, of which £20,000 is accounted for by "Le Cirque."' The excellent catalogue of this show contains the whole history not only of the Neo-Impressionists but also of the Salon des Indépendants, told by Paul Signac, Seurat's friend and follower, who was president of the Salon from 1908 until his death in 1935. He describes the first exhibition held in 1884 in the courtyard of the Tuileries, which the *Figaro* called a 'communist exhibition.' Since then the Indépendants have gradually become the centre of international artistic life, and in 1934 the fiftieth anniversary of the group was celebrated in the Grand Palais.

The first monograph on the Douanier Rousseau was written in 1913 by his friend and earliest buyer, Wilhelm Uhde. Uhde was unable to find a publisher for it in France or elsewhere, and I issued it myself as the first publication of my newly opened gallery. Many books on Rousseau, sumptuously printed and illustrated, made their appearance after the War, when the rue la Boétie took possession of his work and pushed up his prices, but I doubt if any of them are as charming and valuable as Uhde's little volume.

Albums of reproductions of the nineteenth-century masters have been published in all countries, including the splendid portfolios of the Marées Society, with their excellent facsimiles of water colours, the first of which, devoted to Cézanne, appeared during the War. Big firms now publish colour reproductions of the most important pictures and sell them at prices within the means of all; they are bought as our grandfathers bought engravings of the Sistine Madonna or fox-hunting prints. The Impressionists are now as popular with the general public as Rubens or Raphael, as the English portraitists or sporting painters.

Yet the best books on the subject have probably been written by the artists themselves. There are the *Journal* of Delacroix, for instance, the *Letters* of Van Gogh, and the *Noa Noa* and *Avant et Après* by Gauguin. There are *Les Cathédrales* by Rodin and Signac's *D'Eugène Delacroix au Néo-Impréssionisme*.

What more can I add to what I have written? What explanations, what criticisms, what philosophy to prove that from the standpoint of art this French nineteenth century is veritably the *Grand Siècle*?

III

On plaisante facilement sur les œuvres d'art nouveaux ; cela dispense de les comprendre.
GUILLAUME APOLLINAIRE.

(1) *Eighty Years Ago: 1855.*

'I have just been to see the Courbet Exhibition. I found his refused picture ("L'Atelier") a masterpiece. I could hardly tear myself away from it. It shows enormous progress, and even brings me to admire his "Enterrement" . . . They have refused one of the most remarkable pictures of the age.' EUGÈNE DELACROIX in his *Journal, August 3rd*, 1855.

(2) *Sixty Years Ago: 1876.*

'A fate seems to attach to the rue Peletier nowadays. After the fire at the Opera, a new disaster has overtaken the district. An exhibition has just opened at the Durand-Ruel Gallery which purports to be of painting. The inoffensive passer-by, attracted by the posters which decorate the frontage, enters, and a strange sight strikes his astonished eyes; five or six lunatics, one of them a woman—a collection of unfortunates tainted by the folly of ambition—have met here to exhibit their works.

'There are people who can simply laugh these things away. I am not one of them; they tear at my heart. These so-called artists call themselves the advance-guard, impressionists. They take hold of canvas, colours, brushes, slap on a few tones and gaily sign the results. It reminds me of the poor half-wits at the Ville-Evrard who pick up chips of stone on the road and think they are diamonds. What a terrifying spectacle is this of human vanity stretched to the verge of dementia. Someone should tell M. Pissarro forcibly that trees are never *violet*, that the sky is never the colour of *fresh butter*, that nowhere on earth are things to be seen as he paints them, and that no intelligence on earth could accept his half-baked conceptions. It would be as much a waste of time as trying to convince a patient of Dr. Blanche, who thinks he is the Pope, that he lives in the Batignolles and not in the Vatican. Let us try now to make M. Degas listen to reason; let us tell him that art consists of certain elements commonly called *design, colour, technique* and *inspiration*; he will burst out laughing in our faces and call us reactionaries. Let us try, then, to explain to M. Renoir that the flesh of a woman is not *a lump of meat in the last stages of decomposition*, with green and violet streaks such as one might think would denote the final putrefaction of a corpse. There is a woman among the group, too, as is the way with all these explosions. She goes by the name of Berthe Morisot, and her methods are worth observing. All womanly dignity seems lost in the outpourings of a soul in delirium.

'This disgusting collection is shown publicly without a thought to the consequences. Yesterday, an unfortunate individual was arrested in the rue Peletier who, on leaving the exhibition, began to bite the passers-by.'

ALBERT WOLFF in *Le Figaro, April 3rd,* 1876.

(3) *Forty Years Ago: 1894-95.*

'We live in an age of decadence and imbecility. I do not speak only from the point of view of Art, no . . . human society itself is losing its balance. . . . Caillebotte? . . . Am I not right in saying that he himself has dabbled in painting? I do not know . . . I know nothing of these gentlemen, and only know of this bequest by hearsay. . . . It includes, I believe, work by M. Monet, and by M. Pissarro, and by some others. I repeat, if the Nation has seen fit to accept this sort of *muck,* what it needs is a complete moral regeneration. . . . This is anarchy, pure and simple, and nothing is done to put an end to it. On the strength of an article by Octave Mirbeau I ventured into Pissarro's exhibition. . . . My bewilderment was complete, it was nothing, nothing. . . . I cannot find words to castigate such an outrage. Nowadays, it seems, all the public requires is eccentricity at any price; some paint one way, others another way; some in dots, others in triangles or what you will. I tell you, these people are nothing but anarchists! and fools!'

JEAN-LÉON GÉRÔME in a letter to the *Journal des Arts* on the acceptance by the French Government of 38 out of the 70 pictures from the Caillebotte collection offered to the Luxembourg. (They are now in the Louvre.)

'I saw trees that no botanist would recognize, beasts that Cuvier would not have dreamt of, and men such as you only have known how to create. There was a sea that seemed to flow from a volcano, a sky that no god would ever dwell in. You have created a new heaven and a new earth.'

AUGUST STRINDBERG, in a letter addressed to Gauguin in 1895 refusing to write a preface for the catalogue of his Exhibition.

(4) *1937.*

The battle is won.

The French Government has even recognized the Douanier Rousseau and accepted 'La Charmeuse de Serpents,' the gift of M. Jacques Doucet, for the Louvre. Maillol's Cézanne Monument stands in the Tuileries Gardens.

No longer are critics and fashionable painters allowed to publish their cheap attacks in the better papers; those who from the first understood the genius of the *Grand Siècle*, and dared to show their admiration publicly, are at last vindicated. Pissarro stands with Hobbema, Manet with Goya, Renoir with Rubens. The revolutionaries of yesterday are the classics of today; the fighting is forgotten, and people hardly remember that any fighting took place at all. Gone is the day when those who wished to study the Impressionists could only do so in the dark *Musée des Arts Decoratifs*, in the small entrance room of the Luxembourg, at a few dealers such as Durand-Ruel, Bernheim, Vollard, Rosenberg and Paul Guillaume, Apollinaire's friend; or in the private collections of Durand-Ruel and Auguste Pellerin (who had exchanged his Manets for Cézannes) in the rue de Rome and of Alphonse Kann in the Avenue du Bois. The Louvre has now united its treasures—the Moreau-Nelaton and Caillebotte collections, and its other gifts. They hang proudly in a good light, and perhaps before long the Camondo collection will be moved to a place near these rooms so that the whole *Grand Siècle* may be brought together, or, better still, housed in a special gallery built for the purpose.

But the Paris of today is not the pre-War Paris. It was beautiful and young, that pre-War Paris, full of fight and struggle, an art centre of the world in which the approaching triumph of the Impressionists was stimulating a new generation, the Fauves and the Impressionists, to fiercer action. Every lover of art, European or American, serious or snob, collector, writer or painter, would spend a few days there, a few months, or a few years. For the time, at least, he became a Parisian. He enjoyed and criticized the exhibitions at the Salon d'Automne, at the Indépendants, at the dealers. He enjoyed King Sisowath and his Cambodian Dancers, who so delighted Rodin, and the triumphant entry of Russia into Europe with Diaghelev, Nijinsky, Stravinsky and Pavlova. He enjoyed Maxim's, and Montmartre with Père Fred and Pascin and Utrillo, the Clôserie des Lilas, the Deux Magots and Montparnasse. There, at the Café du Dôme, *le cerveau du monde*, he entered into discussions lasting from morning till deep into the night, on the subject of who was the greater, Cézanne or Van Gogh—just as later the odds would be placed between Matisse and Picasso.

The discussions are over. Paris seems middle-aged and self-satisfied, and speaks less about pictures than about prices. Everyone is an art-dealer nowadays, whether he understands anything about art or about business. Montmartre is dead and the Café du Dôme a Babel, where, to use Vollard's words, the painters for the most part talk in terms of dollars, piastres, pesetas, kroner or pound sterling, rather than in terms of art.

The rue Laffitte has been pulled down. Durand-Ruel has moved to the neighbourhood of the Champs Élysées, and Vollard himself has bought an *hôtel* in the fashionable Faubourg St. Germain, where he publishes luxurious books and for the last ten years has been preparing his great exhibition of the works of Degas. The rue la Boétie has become a Throgmorton Street of Art, with branches in New York and, since Berlin's defection, in Bond Street.

IV

It is useless to protest that great art does not speak an international language, but it is right to protest against the work of second- or third-rate men (who may be none the less artists for that) being artificially elevated to its level—simply, perhaps, because they are French. An art which is in its nature provincial or national can never aspire to the international level. What do you in England know of Segantini, for instance, whom the Italians consider one of their most important painters, or of Sorolla, the best Impressionist of Spain? What do Italians or Spaniards know of Duncan Grant or John? When such artists seek an international, rather than a national, reputation, it is liable to break down in the exportation—as does so often the *haute couture* of other countries when it tries to emulate the creations of Lanvin or Scaparelli.

Art need be none the worse for being national or provincial, but really great art soars above racial frontiers and belongs to the world. Thus it was with the best in French Art during the *Grand Siècle*. Such an art, to borrow J. B. Manson's words, 'can be understood with few exceptions by the whole world. It affords a common meeting ground, and transcends all those considerations of Imperialism and politics which are the cause of international strife and ill will.'

INDEX

(The numerals in italics denote the *figure numbers* of illustrations.)

A Selected List of
BATSFORD BOOKS
relating to

Architecture, Fine and Decorative Art, Social History, The Countryside, Church Art, Interior Decoration, Design and Ornament, Crafts, etc.

Published by B. T. BATSFORD LTD

Booksellers and Publishers by Appointment to H.M. Queen Mary

15 North Audley Street, Mayfair
London, W 1

CONTENTS

NOTE.—This list comprises over 250 books on the subjects shown above from Batsford's main catalogue, in which are listed some 600 odd titles. It is intended to form a representative selection for the use of readers, but those interested in any particular subject should obtain the main catalogue (which will be sent post free on request), that comprises a much wider range of titles under every head. Fully illustrated prospectuses of most books can also be sent on request. Patrons are reminded that Batsford's new premises are at 15 North Audley Street, London, W.1, one minute from Oxford Street, on the main thoroughfare leading to Grosvenor Square, three minutes' walk from either Bond Street or Marble Arch Stations on the Central London Railway; there an immense stock of books, old and new, English and foreign, with prints, pictures, etc., can be inspected at leisure in the large and beautifully-fitted showrooms and gallery. *Telephone Mayfair 6118. Cables: Batsfordia, London. Telegrams: Batsford, Audley, London.*

List G. 50m. 3/37.

THE LAND OF WALES

By EILUNED and PETER LEWIS. A Pictorial Review of Welsh Scenery and Life, with chapters on the Countryside, the Towns, Sport, Religion, the Spirit of Wales, etc. Written by a Welsh brother and sister, both of whom have made names for themselves in literary spheres, the book forms the best introduction yet issued to Wales and the Welsh. With 130 superb photographic illustrations, and a colour Frontispiece. Demy 8vo, cloth. 7s. 6d. net.

THE OLD TOWNS OF ENGLAND

By CLIVE ROUSE, F.S.A. A Review of their Types and History, Features and Industries, including Cathedral Cities, Spas and Resorts, Market Towns, Scholastic and Church Centres, Sea Ports, etc. Illustrated by some 120 fine photographs of public and private buildings, picturesque byways, aerial views, etc. With coloured Frontispiece. Demy 8vo, cloth. 7s. 6d. net.

ENGLISH VILLAGE HOMES

By SYDNEY R. JONES, author of "Touring England," etc. With a Foreword by SIR W. BEACH THOMAS. An historical and comparative review of many types of Country Buildings, including the Farm, Cottage, Inn, Manor, Rectory, Cross, Lock-up, etc. Illustrated by some 130 fine photographs, many sketches and drawings and a coloured Frontispiece. Demy 8vo, cloth. 7s. 6d. net.

THE ENGLISH CASTLE

By HUGH BRAUN, F.S.A., A.R.I.B.A. A review of the origin, evolution and vicissitudes of medieval fortresses, with accounts of military engines, famous sieges, etc. Illustrated by a coloured Frontispiece and some 125 fine photographs of general and air views, features and details of the outstanding examples in England and Wales. Demy 8vo, cloth. 7s. 6d. net.

THE SEAS AND SHORES OF ENGLAND

By EDMUND VALE. An interesting account of the varied English and Welsh coastline, its Cliffs and Coves, Estuaries and Ports, Inlets and Harbours, including the Solway, the Irish Sea and St. George's Channel, the Severn Sea, the Atlantic, the English Channel and the North Sea. Illustrated by 130 photographs and a coloured Frontispiece. Demy 8vo, cloth. 7s. 6d. net.

THE ENGLISH COUNTRY HOUSE

By RALPH DUTTON. An historical and social review, tracing design and evolution from the Conquest to Victorian times, including Interior Decoration and Gardens. Illustrated by 130 fine Photographs of Medieval, Elizabethan, Stuart, Georgian, Classic and Neo-Gothic examples. With coloured Frontispiece and numerous plans. Demy 8vo, cloth. 7s. 6d. net.

THE ENGLISH ABBEY: ITS LIFE & WORK IN THE MIDDLE AGES.

By FRED H. CROSSLEY, F.S.A. With a Foreword by the Rt. Hon. W. Ormsby-Gore, P.C., M.P. An informative review of Origins and Orders, the Working Staff of the Convent, the Buildings, Daily Round and Processions, Administration, Building Methods and Social Reactions. With 138 illustrations from photographs of interior and exterior views, features, etc., a map, numerous plans, and 3 coloured plates. Demy 8vo, cloth. 7s. 6d. net.

THE PARISH CHURCHES OF ENGLAND

By the Rev. J. C. COX, LL.D. With a Foreword by the VERY REV. W. R. INGE, D.D., late Dean of St. Paul's. With Chapters on the Life and Services, the Evolution of Plan, Structural Design, Fittings and Furniture, and Local Varieties of Style. Including 135 fine photographic illustrations, also plans and drawings. With coloured Frontispiece. Demy 8vo, cloth. 7s. 6d. net.

THE "BRITISH HERITAGE" SERIES—(continued)

THE FACE OF SCOTLAND

A Pictorial Review of its Scenery: Hills, Glens, Lochs, Coast, Islands Moors, etc., with Old Buildings, Castles, Churches, etc. Including a brief review of Topography, History and Characteristics. By HARRY BATSFORD and CHARLES FRY, with a Foreword by JOHN BUCHAN (LORD TWEEDSMUIR). With 130 splendid photographic illustrations, a Frontispiece in colour, and numerous line drawings in the text. Demy 8vo, cloth. 7s. 6d. net.

THE HEART OF SCOTLAND

By GEORGE BLAKE, with a Foreword by ERIC LINKLATER. A companion and complement to "The Face of Scotland." Containing an account of the Land and its People, including a review of Highland Places, the True Lowlands, Black Country, a Tale of Four Cities, the Kirk and the People, the Fireside Clime, Sport, Institutions, Legends and Realities. Containing 130 superb Photographic Illustrations of Scenery and Life, Mountains, Cities, Towns, Sport, etc. With a coloured Frontispiece by KEITH HENDERSON, numerous drawings, and a map. Demy 8vo, cloth. 7s. 6d. net.

Further volumes in the "BRITISH HERITAGE" Series to appear shortly are:

FARMING ENGLAND. By A. G. STREET.

ANCIENT ENGLAND. By EDMUND VALE.

A survey of the Ancient Monuments under the care of H.M. Office of Works and other public bodies.

THE OLD PUBLIC SCHOOLS OF ENGLAND. By JOHN RODGERS.

OLD ENGLISH GARDENS. By RALPH DUTTON.

OLD ENGLISH COUNTRY LIFE. By H. E. BATES.

Price 7s. 6d. net each.

THE "PILGRIMS'" LIBRARY

THE BEAUTY OF BRITAIN

A new composite picture of the English, Welsh and Scottish countryside, under 14 divisions by various writers, with an Introduction by J. B. PRIESTLEY. Including the Coast, and Wales, by EDMUND VALE; the West Country by EDMUND BARBER; the Chalk Country by A. G. STREET; the Central Midlands by SIR W. BEACH THOMAS; Scotland, Lowlands and Highlands, by GEORGE BLAKE; and articles by other well-known writers. Containing 256 pages of text, with 130 splendid photographic pictures and a Frontispiece in colour. Crown 8vo, cloth. 5s. net.

THE LEGACY OF ENGLAND

An Illustrated Survey of the Works of Man in the English Country: Farm, Village, Country House, Town, Church, Inn, Sport. With Introduction by EDMUND BLUNDEN and contributions by ADRIAN BELL, C. BRADLEY FORD, G. M. YOUNG, G. A. BIRMINGHAM, IVOR BROWN and BERNARD DARWIN. 256 pages, illustrated by 130 splendid photographs of examples from all parts. With colour Frontispiece. Crown 8vo, cloth. 5s. net.

NATURE IN BRITAIN

A Pictorial Review of our native wild Fauna and Flora, including Animals, Birds, Fishes and Water Life, Insects, Trees and Shrubs, and Flowers. With Introduction by HENRY WILLIAMSON, and contributions by FRANCES PITT, SETON GORDON, E. G. BOULENGER, C. BUSHBY, R. ST. BARBE BAKER and R. GATHORNE-HARDY. With 120 fine photographs and colour Frontispiece. Crown 8vo, cloth. 5s. net.

5

THE "FACE OF BRITAIN" SERIES

NORTH COUNTRY

By EDMUND VALE. A Pictorial Survey of Northumberland, Durham, Cumberland, Westmorland, Lancashire and Yorkshire, rural and industrial, with an account of its life in town and country, ranging from the remote sheep-farming of the Pennines to the coal, steel and textile activities of the great manufacturing areas. A chapter on "No Man's Land" deals acutely with the problem of the Distressed Areas, while about 130 illustrations reveal every aspect of Northern life and scenery. With a Frontispiece in colour. Demy 8vo, cloth. 7s. 6d. net.

THE FACE OF IRELAND

By MICHAEL FLOYD. A vivid and human survey of Irish Scenery and Life. Splendidly illustrated by over 130 Photographs, for the most part specially taken by WILL F. TAYLOR. After a general Introduction, the country is treated under five broad divisions: Dublin, Wicklow and the South-East, Kerry and the South-West, Connemara and the Mid-West, Donegal and the North-East, the Six Counties, Central Ireland. The illustrations form, perhaps, the finest series ever devoted to their subject. Mr. PAUL HENRY contributes a colour Frontispiece. Demy 8vo, cloth. 7s. 6d. net.

THE HIGHLANDS OF SCOTLAND

By HUGH QUIGLEY. A graphic account of the Cairngorms, the Lower Grampians, the Far North-West, the West Coast, the Inner and Outer Hebrides and the Glencoe district. Illustrated by some 130 fine Photographs of mountains, lochs, seascapes, rivers, glens, woods, etc., by ROBERT M. ADAM. With coloured Frontispiece by W. DOUGLAS MCLEOD, Maps, etc. Demy 8vo, cloth. 7s. 6d. net.

ENGLISH DOWNLAND

By H. J. MASSINGHAM, Author of "Wold Without End," "Downland Man," etc. A comprehensive review of the features, distinctive characteristics, antiquities, villages, etc., of the Chalk Country in England, including the Wiltshire Mass, the Berkshire Ridges, the Chilterns, the North and South Downs, etc. Illustrated by 130 fine photographs of general views, hill-scenes, panoramas, farms and fieldwork, cottages and churches, barrows, cromlechs, etc. With a Frontispiece in colour. Demy 8vo, cloth. 7s. 6d. net.

Forthcoming additions to the "FACE OF BRITAIN" Series include:

COTSWOLD COUNTRY. By H. J. MASSINGHAM.

THE ISLANDS OF SCOTLAND. By H. M'DIARMID.

THE WELSH BORDER COUNTRY. By P. T. JONES. 7s. 6d. net each.

HUNTING ENGLAND

By SIR WILLIAM BEACH THOMAS, author of "Village England," etc. A survey of the sport and its chief grounds. With accounts of every leading pack and the country over which it hunts. Illustrated by 10 plates in colour (some double) from old paintings and prints by renowned artists, and over 100 subjects from photographs. Demy 8vo, cloth. 7s. 6d. net.

THE ISLANDS OF IRELAND

By THOMAS H. MASON. A racy, first-hand account, in text and pictures of their scenery, peoples, antiquities and primitive life, illustrated by some 140 reproductions of specially taken photographs of the Arans, Blaskets, Tory, Clare and other islands, including prehistoric forts, Christian antiquities, currachs, interiors, peasant types, etc. With a Frontispiece in colour. Large 8vo, cloth. 10s. 6d. net.

BATSFORD'S "ART AND LIFE IN COLOUR" LIBRARY

In two sizes: (I) Quarto (II) Small Folio. (I) comprises BEAUTY OF
TROPICAL BUTTERFLIES; WONDERS OF THE SEA: SHELLS;
THE SEASONS OF THE YEAR in Masterpieces of Flemish Illumina-
tion; to be followed by TYPICAL MINERALS and ALPINE FLOWERS.
Each contains 12 superb facsimile colour plates, reproduced regardless of
expense, forming veritable works of art. With brief Introduction and text.
Stiff covers, 5s. 6d. per volume.
II. PAINTING OF THE FAR EAST, chiefly Chinese, with some Japanese
examples; the LANDSCAPES OF SWITZERLAND from views of a
century ago; to be followed by OLD STAINED GLASS and LIFE OF
THE SEA. With brief introductions and text. 7s. 6d. net per volume.
These two sister series constitute an endeavour to represent some of the
finest works of Nature and Art by the highest achievements of modern
colour processes. No trouble or cost has been stinted to obtain most
artistic facsimile results, which will appeal to all for their beauty and
intrinsic interest. Copies in portfolio can be supplied for framing if wished.
The introductions on Butterflies, Shells and Life of the Sea are by
Professor Julian Huxley, F.S.A., of the London Zoo; that of the volume on
Illumination by Mr. Francis Kelly, the writer on costume; and to the
volume on Painting of the Far East by Mr. Laurence Binyon,
the well-known authority on Oriental Art.

THE "ENGLISH LIFE" SERIES

THE MEDIEVAL STYLES OF THE ENGLISH PARISH CHURCH

By F. E. Howard, joint author of "English Church Woodwork," etc. A
careful and informative account of the Evolution of Design, Features and
Detail from early pre-Conquest days to the sixteenth century, including
chapters on each Transitional Phase and on Methods of Studying a Parish
Church. With 180 illustrations from photographs of exterior and
interior views, etc., plans and mouldings. Large 8vo, cloth. 12s. 6d. net.

THE ENGLISH COUNTRYSIDE

By Ernest C. Pulbrook. A Review of some of its Aspects, Features,
and Attractions. With 126 Illustrations from Photographs, and a Pencil
Frontispiece by A. E. Newcombe. Large 8vo, cloth, gilt. 10s. 6d. net.

ENGLISH COUNTRY LIFE AND WORK

By Ernest C. Pulbrook. Containing about 200 pages on Farmers, Old and
New—Field-Work—Cottage Folk—The Village Craftsman—Religious Life,
etc. With about 200 illustrations from photographs. Large 8vo, cloth, gilt.
12s. 6d. net.

OLD ENGLISH HOUSEHOLD LIFE

By Gertrude Jekyll. Consisting of 17 sections on the Fireplace, Candle-
light, the Hearth, the Kitchen, Old Furniture, Home Industries, Cottage
Buildings, Mills, Churchyards, etc. With 277 illustrations from photographs, old prints and drawings. Large 8vo, cloth, gilt. 12s. 6d. net.

THE ENGLISH AT HOME

A graphic pictorial record from photographs specially taken by Bill
Brandt. With an Introduction by Raymond Mortimer. Comprising 64
photogravure plates of typical scenes and Characters at Work and Play
in Town and Country, including Racing, Betting, Mining, Children, rich
and poor, Drinking, Bathing, City Life, Suburbs, a Garden Party, Teas,
high and low, Schools, Games, Sport, etc. 4to, boards, cloth back. 5s. net.

THE QUENNELLS "EVERYDAY LIFE" SERIES

*A Graphic and Popular Survey of the Efforts and Progress of the Human Race
now completed in 4 volumes. Crown 8vo, cloth. 5s. net each.*

I. EVERYDAY LIFE IN THE OLD STONE AGE

Written and Illustrated by MARJORIE and C. H. B. QUENNELL. Containing
128 pages, including 70 Illustrations, and a coloured Frontispiece, from the
Authors' Drawings, with a Chronological Chart. Second Edition, 5s. net.

II. EVERYDAY LIFE IN THE NEW STONE, BRONZE AND EARLY IRON AGES

Written and Illustrated by MARJORIE and C. H. B. QUENNELL. Containing
144 pages, with 90 original Illustrations from the Authors' Drawings, of
Household Life, Agriculture, Pottery, Weapons, etc., including 2 plates in
colour, a map, and a Chronological Chart. Second Edition. 5s. net.

III. EVERYDAY LIFE IN ROMAN BRITAIN

Written and Illustrated by MARJORIE and C. H. B. QUENNELL. Containing
128 pages, with over 100 original Illustrations from the Authors' Pen
Drawings, of Cities and Camps, Villas, Ships, Chariots, Monuments, Costume, Military Life, Household Objects, Pottery, etc. Including 3 Colour
Plates, Chart, and Map of Roads. Second edition, revised. 5s. net.

IV. LIFE IN SAXON, VIKING AND NORMAN TIMES

Written and Illustrated by MARJORIE and C. H. B. QUENNELL. Containing
128 pages, with over 100 original illustrations of Ships, Cooking, Metalwork, Buildings, Pottery, and Illuminated MSS., including 2 coloured
plates, Historical Chart, etc. 5s. net.

THE QUENNELL "CLASSICAL SOCIAL LIFE" SERIES

"The Quennell books are likely to outlast some of the most imposing institutions of the
post-war world. They are written with great scholarship and surprising lucidity.
To speak in superlatives of this series is only justice, for seldom is there found such a unity
between publisher, author, and illustrator as the Batsford books display."—*G.K.'s Weekly.*

VOL I. EVERYDAY THINGS IN HOMERIC GREECE

Written and Illustrated by MARJORIE and C. H. B. QUENNELL. Presenting
a vivid picture based on the Social Life in the Iliad and Odyssey, etc.
Illustrated by 70 Drawings by the Authors, after Vase Paintings and their
own restorations. With Colour Frontispiece, Photographic Illustrations,
Map, etc. Large 8vo, cloth. 7s. 6d. net.

VOL. II. EVERYDAY THINGS IN ARCHAIC GREECE

Written and Illustrated by MARJORIE and C. H. B. QUENNELL. An Account
of Social Life from the close of the Trojan War to the Persian Struggle.
Illustrated by 85 full-page and smaller Drawings by the Authors. With a
coloured Frontispiece, a number of Photographic Illustrations, Map, etc.
Large 8vo, cloth. 7s. 6d. net.

VOL. III. EVERYDAY THINGS IN CLASSICAL GREECE

Written and Illustrated by MARJORIE and C. H. B. QUENNELL. A vivid
picture of Social Life in the Golden Age of Pericles, Socrates, Phidias, and
Plato, 480-404 B.C. With Sections on Architecture; the Town and its
Planning; Everyday Life; Sea Fights and Land Battles, etc. Illustrated by
83 Drawings specially made by the Authors. With coloured Frontispiece,
Photographic Illustrations, Chart, Map, etc. Large 8vo, cloth. 8s. net.

"In their volumes the authors have approached history from a new angle and in the process have revolutionised the teaching of it In their hands it has become a live, vivid and picturesque subject, for they have breathed new life into old bones. Their methods are now widely and generally recognised and appreciated."—*Western Mail.*

A HISTORY OF EVERYDAY THINGS IN ENGLAND

Written and Illustrated by MARJORIE and C. H. B. QUENNELL. In Four Volumes. Medium 8vo, 8s. 6d. net each; also Vols. I and II, and III and IV, issued each pair bound in one volume, 16s. 6d. net.

VOL. I—EVERYDAY THINGS IN ENGLAND, 1066-1499

With 90 Illustrations, many full-page, and 3 Plates in colour. Second Edition, revised and enlarged, with additional illustrations. 8/6 net.

VOL. II—EVERYDAY THINGS IN ENGLAND, 1500-1799

With 4 coloured plates and 111 other illustrations from the Author's Drawings. Second Edition, revised with additional illustrations. 8s. 6d. net.

The above 2 volumes are separately issued in parts for Schools and Class Teaching. Stiff paper covers. Price 3s. net each.

PART I.   ENGLAND UNDER FOREIGN KINGS (1066-1199).
PART II.   THE RISE OF PARLIAMENT (1200-1399).
PART III. THE HUNDRED YEARS' WAR (1400-1499).
PART IV.   THE AGE OF ADVENTURE (1500-1599).
PART V.   THE CROWN'S BID FOR POWER (1600-1699).
PART VI.   THE RISE OF MODERN ENGLAND (1700-1799).

VOL. III—EVERYDAY THINGS IN ENGLAND, 1733-1851

THE COMING OF THE INDUSTRIAL ERA. An Account of the Transition from Traditional to Modern Life and Civilization. Written and Illustrated by MARJORIE and C. H. B. QUENNELL. Tracing the Transformation of Agriculture, the coming of Steam Power, the application of Inventions, Trends in Social Life in Town and Country, Costume, Building, etc. Illustrated by 4 Coloured Plates, 120 full-page and smaller Drawings. Medium 8vo, art cloth. 8s. 6d. net.

VOL. IV.—EVERYDAY THINGS IN ENGLAND, 1852-1934

THE AGE OF PRODUCTION. An Account of Modern Life and Civilisation. Written and Illustrated by MARJORIE and C. H. B. QUENNELL. Treating of old and new methods regarding the Farmer and Food, Buildings, Town Planning, Slums, Schools, Furniture, Production and Distribution, Public Health, Transport, Social Life in Clothes, etc. Illustrated by 4 single and 3 double Plates in colour, 120 full-page and smaller Drawings specially prepared by the authors, and numerous Plates from Photographs and contemporary Prints. Medium 8vo, art cloth. 8s. 6d. net.

THE GOOD NEW DAYS

Things that Boys and Girls Should Know. By MARJORIE and C. H. B. QUENNELL. Demy 8vo, with coloured jacket. 6s. net.

A Series of bright informative talks about the fundamental factors of English Citizenship, present-day conditions and problems, and including comparisons with the past, in Agriculture, Towns and Suburbs, Trade and Finance, Production, Legislation, Leisure, Taxation, National Debt and Imprisonment, Armaments, etc., With historical summaries. Illustrated by numerous plans, diagrams, old prints and up-to-date photographs.

A striking and original book, which provides a stimulating course in English Civics.

9

THE "PEOPLE'S LIFE AND WORK" SERIES

LIFE AND WORK OF THE ENGLISH PEOPLE THROUGH THE CENTURIES

A Pictorial Record from Contemporary Sources. By DOROTHY HARTLEY and MARGARET M. ELLIOT, B.A. (Lond.). Each volume is devoted to a century and contains about 150 pictures on 48 Plates, of Household Life, Industries, Building, Farming, Warfare, Transport, Children, Church Life, Gardens, etc. With an Introduction, Descriptive Notes, Chart, Analytical Index, Music, etc. Large (royal) 8vo, boards, lettered, or in portfolio with flaps, 3s. net, or in cloth, 3s. 6d. net per volume.

The Series has now been completed as follows:

I. SAXON TIMES TO 1300	IV. THE SIXTEENTH CENTURY
II. THE FOURTEENTH CENTURY	V. THE SEVENTEENTH CENTURY
III. THE FIFTEENTH CENTURY	VI. THE EIGHTEENTH CENTURY

Volumes I and II (Early Middle Ages), III and IV (Later Middle Ages), and V and VI (Renaissance) are also issued bound together in cloth to form 3 vols., 6s. net each; and Volumes I, II and III (Middle Ages), and IV, V and VI (Renaissance) are also bound in cloth to form 2 vols., at 9s. net each.

THE "ESSENTIALS OF LIFE" SERIES

By Lieut.-Colonel F. S. BRERETON, C.B.E. Bright, informative reviews of the Indispensable Things of Human Life. Each with 80 pages of text, and about 100 Illustrations in Line and Half-tone from Photographs, Drawings, Old Prints, etc., of Old and Modern Developments. Large crown 8vo, cloth. Cheaper reissue. 2s. 6d. net each.

CLOTHING: An Account of its Types and Manufacture. Contents: Materials — Spinning — Weaving — The Sewing Machine — A Morden Factory—Furs and Rubber—Leather and Tanning—Boots—Hats—Glove-making—Dyeing and Cleaning—Pins—Needles—Buttons, etc.

TRAVEL: An Account of its Methods in Past and Present. Contents: Early Roads and Trading Routes—Coaching—The Steam Engine—Steamships and Railways—The Bicycle—The Petrol Engine—Air Travel —Postman—Wire or Wireless. With Illustrations of Coaches, Engines, Balloons, Aircraft, Ships, Steamers, etc.

ENGLAND IN TUDOR TIMES

An Account of its Social Life and Industries. By L. F. SALZMAN, M.A. F.S.A. With 138 pages of text, 64 full-page plates and numerous illustrations in the text. Demy 8vo, cloth. 5s.

TOURING LONDON

By W. TEIGNMOUTH SHORE. With an introduction by the Rt. Hon. John Burns, P.C. A Series of 4 Tours, covering the chief parts of Inner London, illustrated by 28 photographs, drawings and sketches, also a map of the City. Crown 8vo, cloth. 2s. 6d. net.

TOURING ENGLAND BY ROAD AND BY-WAY

A Popular Illustrated Guide, in a new form, to the Beauties of Rural England. By SYDNEY R. JONES. Comprising 20 Typical Tours under Five Divisions, with General Introduction and complete Map, Introduction to each District and specially drawn simplified Route Map of each Tour, which is described in detail, with finger-post reference to features, and buildings of Interest. Illustrated by 54 drawings and 50 photographs. Crown 8vo. 5s. net.

MASKS OF THE WORLD

A COMPREHENSIVE, COMPARATIVE SURVEY OF THE PRODUCTIONS OF MANY PEOPLES AND PERIODS. By JOSEF GREGOR, Director of the Theatrical Art Section, National Library, Vienna. With an Historical and Cultural Introduction and 255 Illustrations finely reproduced in collotype from specially taken Photographs, including 15 subjects in full colour. Comprising striking examples, with some complete robes, from primitive tribes in North and South America, Africa; the Far East; Ancient Greece and Rome; Renaissance France and Italy; and Modernist designers. Edition limited to 200 English copies. Small folio. Art linen, gilt. £6 6s. net.

MEDIEVAL COSTUME AND LIFE

An Historic and Practical Review. By DOROTHY HARTLEY. Containing 22 full-page Plates from Photographs of living Male and Female Figures in specially made Costumes from Medieval MSS., 20 Plates in Line from the Author's Drawings of practical Construction, Detail, Sketches, etc., and 40 Plates of some 200 Reproductions from Contemporary Manuscripts of scenes of Medieval life and work. Including full historical and descriptive text, with directions for the practical cutting out and making of many costumes illustrated. Large royal 8vo, cloth. 12s. net.

A SHORT HISTORY OF COSTUME AND ARMOUR, CHIEFLY IN ENGLAND, 1066-1800

By F. M. KELLY and RANDOLPH SCHWABE, Principal of the Slade School of Fine Art. Royal 8vo, cloth, gilt. 25s. net. Or in 2 volumes:

I. THE MIDDLE AGES, 1066-1485. With Sections on Civilian Dress, "Shirts," "Shapes," Houppelandes and Burgundian Modes Armour. Illustrated by 4 Plates in colours and gold, over 100 Pen Drawings and 32 Photographic Plates. Royal 8vo, cloth, gilt. 13s. net.

II. THE RENAISSANCE, 1485-1800. With Sections on Puff and Slashes, The Spanish Trend, "Cavalier" and French Modes, the Heyday and Decline of Powder, Armour, etc. Illustrated by 5 Plates (3 double) in colours and gold, over 100 Pen Drawings and 36 Photographic Plates of 58 Reproductions. Royal 8vo, cloth, gilt. 13s. net.

HISTORICAL COSTUME

A Chronicle of Fashion in Western Europe, 1490-1790. By FRANCIS M. KELLY and RANDOLPH SCHWABE. Containing the chief characteristics of Dress in each century. Illustrated by some hundreds of full-page and text Sketches from original sources by RANDOLPH SCHWABE of typical groups, figures and details. Including 7 Plates specially reproduced in colour, and 70 Photographic reproductions of Pictures, Portraits, Scenes, etc. Second Edition revised and enlarged. Large royal 8vo, cloth, gilt. 25s. net.

SHAKESPEARE'S "ROMEO AND JULIET"

With designs for Costumes and Stage Settings by OLIVER MESSEL. A beautiful edition of this famous tragedy, decoratively printed, containing 96 pages of text, 8 colour and 32 monochrome collotype Plates of the designs specially made for the Metro-Goldwyn-Mayer Film Production. Special limited edition. Demy 4to, decorative cloth and colour jacket. 21s. net.

CHILDREN'S TOYS OF BYGONE DAYS

A History of Playthings of all Peoples from Prehistoric Times to the XIXth Century. By KARL GRÖBER. English Version by PHILIP HEREFORD. A beautifully produced survey, with a Frontispiece and 11 Plates in colour, and 306 photographic illustrations of Dolls, Dolls-houses, Mechanical Toys, Carts, Ships, Tin Soldiers, etc., of every country and period. 4to canvas, gilt. New and cheaper edition, 12s. 6d. net.

A HISTORY OF ARCHITECTURE ON THE COMPARATIVE METHOD FOR THE STUDENT, CRAFTSMAN AND AMATEUR

By Sir Banister Fletcher, PP.R.I.B.A., F.S.A. Ninth Edition, completely rewritten. Containing over 1,000 pages, with about 4,000 Illustrations (1,560 recently added and nearly 2,000 reproduced larger) from Photographs of Buildings and from specially arranged comparative Drawings of Structures, Plans, Detail and Ornament. Royal 8vo, cloth, gilt. £2 2s. net.

"A wonderful storehouse of accurate information enriched by an amazing wealth of illustrations. Author and publisher alike are to be congratulated on a remarkable achievement."—*The Journal of the Royal Institute of British Architects.*

BATSFORD'S "HISTORICAL ARCHITECTURE" LIBRARY
of Standard Textbooks on Classic and Renaissance Architecture

ARCHITECTURE OF GREECE AND ROME

By W. J. Anderson and R. Phene Spiers. Now reissued in two volumes, obtainable separately, revised and much enlarged. Medium 8vo, cloth, gilt. 21s. net each volume, or £2 the two.

I. ARCHITECTURE OF ANCIENT GREECE. Rewritten, remodelled and much enlarged by William Bell Dinsmoor, Professor of Architecture at Columbia University, New York, and the American Academy at Athens. With over 200 Illustrations in Collotype, half-tone and line.

II. ARCHITECTURE OF ANCIENT ROME. Revised and rewritten by Thomas Ashby, LL.D., Late Director of the British School at Rome. With about 200 Illustrations in half-tone and line.

BYZANTINE ARCHITECTURE AND DECORATION

By J. Arnott Hamilton, M.A., author of "The Churches of Palermo," etc. A careful, scholarly and thorough account of the development and character of constructional methods and decoration, and types of extant buildings in Constantinople, Greece, the Balkans, Cyprus, Armenia, Italy, etc. With coloured Frontispiece and 120 Photographic Illustrations of exteriors and interiors, Constructional Diagrams, Carving, Details, etc., and numerous Line Drawings. Medium 8vo, cloth, gilt. 18s. net.

ARCHITECTURE OF THE RENAISSANCE IN ITALY

By William J. Anderson, A.R.I.B.A. Revised and Enlarged, with an additional Chapter on Baroque and later work, by Arthur Stratton, F.S.A., F.R.I.B.A. With 80 Plates, including 16 in Collotype, and 120 Illustrations in the text. Medium 8vo, cloth, gilt. 21s. net.

ARCHITECTURE OF THE RENAISSANCE IN FRANCE

By W. H. Ward, M.A., F.R.I.B.A. Revised and Enlarged by Sir John W. Simpson, K.B.E., PP.R.I.B.A. In two volumes, obtainable separately. Medium 8vo, cloth, gilt. 21s. net, each volume, or £2 for the two.
IV. THE EARLY RENAISSANCE (1495-1640). With 259 Illustrations.
V. THE LATER RENAISSANCE (1640-1830). With 214 Illustrations.

The following new volume in the Historical Architecture Library will appear shortly:

A HISTORY OF SPANISH ARCHITECTURE FROM THE EARLIEST TIMES TO THE NINETEENTH CENTURY. By Bernard Bevan, M.A. Profusely illustrated by photographs, drawings and plans. Medium 8vo, cloth. Price 21s. net (approx.).

A SHORT CRITICAL HISTORY OF ARCHITECTURE

By H. HEATHCOTE STATHAM, F.R.I.B.A. Second Edition, revised and enlarged by G. MAXWELL AYLWIN, F.R.I.B.A. Containing 600 pages and 750 Illustrations from Photographs, Drawings, Plans, Prints, etc., with Chronological Charts and Glossary. Demy 8vo, cloth, gilt. 16s. net.

Also supplied in 3 parts, cloth, gilt. 6s. net each.

I. Architecture of Antiquity and the Classic Ages
II. Byzantine, Romanesque and Saracenic Styles
III. The Middle Ages and the Renaissance to Modern Times.

" Within the limits of its size and price it is the most valuable handbook that has appeared in English for those who wish to understand the architecture of the past." —*The Architect.*

THE STORY OF ARCHITECTURE

From the Earliest Ages to the Present Day. By P. LESLIE WATERHOUSE, F.R.I.B.A. With 131 Illustrations of the great buildings of all time from Photographs and Drawings, and many Diagrams in the text of Plans, Views and features. F'cap 8vo, boards. 6s. net.

THE STORY OF ARCHITECTURE IN ENGLAND

By WALTER H. GODFREY, F.S.A., F.R.I.B.A. A popular illustrated account, in which the aims and methods of Architectural Design are simply explained, and linked up with the social life of the time. In Two Parts: I. Early and Medieval, to 1500, chiefly Churches; II. Renaissance, 1500-1800, chiefly Houses. Demy 8vo, cloth. 6s. 6d. net per part.

I. PRE-REFORMATION, THE PERIOD OF CHURCH BUILDING
Illustrated by 133 photographs and drawings. 6s. 6d. net.
II. RENAISSANCE, THE PERIOD OF HOUSE BUILDING
Illustrated by 150 photographs and drawings. 6s. 6d. net.

ENGLISH GOTHIC CHURCHES

THE STORY OF THEIR ARCHITECTURE. By CHARLES W. BUDDEN, M.A. A simple informative account of the Planning, Design, and Details of Parish Churches, Cathedrals, etc., 1066-1500, including Chapters on Local Building, Towers, Spires, Ornaments, etc. Illustrated by 53 Plans and Line Diagrams, and 40 Photographic Plates of 80 Views and Details, including a County List of the chief Churches worth seeing. Crown 8vo, cloth, 5s. net.

ENGLAND'S GREATER CHURCHES

A Pictorial Record with an Introduction and Descriptive Notes by C. B. NICOLSON. Containing 100 Illustrations of general and detail views, exterior and interior, of Cathedrals, Abbeys, Collegiate Churches and Chapels, etc. Square 8vo, 4to cloth, pictorial sides. 3s. 6d. net.

THE ENGLISH HOME FROM CHARLES I TO GEORGE IV

By J. ALFRED GOTCH, F.S.A. A Review of the development of House Building, Decoration and Garden Design from Early Stuart times to the commencement of the XIXth Century. Containing 300 Illustrations, showing Decoration, Panelling, Gardens, Iron and Lead Work, Street Lay-outs, Shop Fronts, etc., etc. Large 8vo, cloth, gilt. 30s. net.

THE GROWTH OF THE ENGLISH HOUSE

A short History of its Design and Development from 1100 to 1800 A.D. By J. ALFRED GOTCH, F.S.A., PP.R.I.B.A. Containing 300 pages, with over 150 Illustrations from Photographs, and many pictures in the text from Measured Drawings, Sketches, Plans, and Old Prints. Second Edition, revised and enlarged. Large crown 8vo, cloth, gilt 12s. 6d. net.

THE DOMESTIC ARCHITECTURE OF ENGLAND DURING THE TUDOR PERIOD

Illustrated in a Series of Photographs and Measured Drawings of Country Houses, Manor Houses and Other Buildings. By THOMAS GARNER and ARTHUR STRATTON, F.R.I.B.A. Second Edition, Revised and Enlarged, comprising 210 Plates, mostly full-page, finely reproduced in Collotype, and 250 pages of Historical and Descriptive Text, including 462 Illustrations of Additional Views, Plans, Details, etc., from photographs and drawings, making a total of over 800 Illustrations in all. In two volumes, small folio, buckram, gilt. £9 9s. net the set. (The volumes cannot be obtained separately but *the set can be purchased by instalments.*)

THE SMALLER ENGLISH HOUSE FROM 1660-1840

By A. E. RICHARDSON, A.R.A., F.R.I.B.A., and HAROLD DONALDSON EBERLEIN, B.A. Treating of the Characteristics and Periods of Style; the Evolution of Plan; Materials and Craftsmanship: Roofing, Windows, Ironwork, Fireplaces, Staircases, Wall Treatment, Ceilings. With over 200 illustrations from photographs and drawings. Demy 4to, cloth. 15s. net.

THE OLD HALLS AND MANOR HOUSES OF NORTH-AMPTONSHIRE

By J. ALFRED GOTCH, M.A., F.S.A., F.R.I.B.A. With full Historical Introduction and descriptive text, and 100 plates of some 150 illustrations from photographs, original drawings and old prints, comprising Interior and Exterior Views, Features, Plans, Details and Gardens. Crown 4to, cloth. 21s. net.

THE STYLES OF ENGLISH ARCHITECTURE

A SERIES OF COMPARATIVE WALL OR LECTURE DIAGRAMS. For Schools, Teachers, Students, etc. By ARTHUR STRATTON, F.S.A., F.R.I.B.A.

Series I: THE MIDDLE AGES (Saxon Times to the Start of the Tudor Period). Consisting of 13 diagrams, 20in. by 30in. 13s. net on stout paper, or 32s. net mounted on linen.

Series II: THE RENAISSANCE (Tudor, Elizabethan, Stuart, and Georgian Periods). Comprising 12 diagrams. 12s. net paper, or 30s. net mounted.

An Introductory Handbook to each series is issued, containing reduced reproductions of all the plates, and an outline account of each style with further illustrations. Paper covers 1s. 6d. net; cloth 2s. 6d. net each.

GEORGIAN ENGLAND (1700-1830)

A Review of its Social Life, Arts and Industries. By Professor A. E. RICHARDSON, A.R.A., F.R.I.B.A. Containing sections on the Social Scene, Navy, Army, Church, Sport, Architecture, Building Crafts, the Trades, Decorative Arts, Painting, Literature, Theatres, etc. Illustrated by 200 subjects from Photographs and contemporary Prints, Engravings and Drawings. With 54 Line Text Illustrations, and a Colour Frontispiece. Medium 8vo, cloth, gilt. 21s. net.

THE XVIIITH CENTURY IN LONDON

An Account of its Social Life and Arts. By E. BERESFORD CHANCELLOR. Containing 280 pages, with 192 illustrations from prints and contemporary drawings and a Frontispiece in colour. 4to, cloth, gilt. 15s. net.

LIFE IN REGENCY AND EARLY VICTORIAN TIMES

An Account of Social Life in the days of Brummel and D'Orsay (1800-1843). By E. BERESFORD CHANCELLOR. With numerous illustrations from rare prints and original drawings. Large 8vo, cloth, gilt. 12s. 6d. net.

FORM AND DESIGN IN CLASSIC ARCHITECTURE

By Arthur Stratton, F.S.A., F.R.I.B.A. Presenting in 80 Plates from Measured Drawings, 600 motives of Façades, Halls, Colonnades, Staircases, etc., selected from fine representative buildings shown in Plan, Elevation and Section. 4to, cloth, gilt. 28s. net.

"This beautiful book is a most welcome addition to the library of architecture. Nothing could be simpler or more logical; yet it gives us an idea of the variety, complexity, and beauty of this classic architecture."—*Journal of the Royal Institute of British Architects.*

THE ORDERS OF ARCHITECTURE

Greek, Roman, and Renaissance; with examples of their historic Application in Italian, French, English, and American Buildings. By Arthur Stratton, F.S.A. With an Introduction by A. Trystan Edwards, A.R.I.B.A. Illustrated in a series of 80 plates from specially prepared drawings, including a complete series of Vignola's Orders, and rendered examples of French, Italian, and English buildings. With full historical and practical notes. 4to, bound in cloth, gilt, or in portfolio, 21s. net; or in 3 parts: CLASSIC, ITALIAN, and APPLICATIONS, cloth 8s. net each.

RENAISSANCE PALACES OF NORTHERN ITALY

(With some Buildings of Earlier Periods). From the XIIIth to the XVIIth Centuries. Edited by Professor Dr. Albrecht Haupt, in 3 vols., each containing 160 full-page Plates in Collotype from specially taken Photographs or Measured Drawings. With full text. Vol. I, TUSCANY, Florence, Pisa, Siena, Montepulciano, Lucca, Pistoia, etc.; Vol. II, VENICE, including also Verona, Mantua, Vicenza, and Padua; Vol. III, GENOA, including also Bologna, Ferrara, Modena, Milan, Turin, Pavia, Bergamo, Brescia, etc. Small folio, cloth, £2 15s. net each volume, or the set of 3 for £7 10s. net.

EARLY CHURCH ART IN NORTHERN EUROPE

With special Reference to Timber Construction and Decoration. By Professor Josef Strzygowski, Author of "Origin of Christian Church Art," etc. Dealing with Pre-Romanesque Art of the Croatians; Wooden Architecture in Eastern Europe; Half-Timber Churches in Western Europe; The Mast Churches of Norway; Royal Tombs in Scandinavia. With 190 Illustrations. Royal 8vo, cloth, gilt. 21s. net.

ART IN THE LIFE OF MANKIND

A Survey of its Achievements from the Earliest Times. By Allen W. Seaby. Planned in a series of concise volumes, each containing about 80 pages of text, with about 70 illustrations from the author's drawings, and a series of 16 photographic plates. Crown 8vo, cloth. 5s. net per volume.

I. A GENERAL VIEW OF ART: Its Nature, Meaning, Principles and Appreciation. II. THE ART OF ANCIENT TIMES (Egypt, Chaldæa, Assyria, Persia, and other lands). III. GREEK ART. IV. ROMAN AND BYZANTINE ART.

These volumes are designed to serve as an Introduction to the Appreciation and Study of Art in general. They are simply written and fully illustrated.

A SHORT HISTORY OF ART

From Prehistoric times to the Nineteenth Century. Translated from the French of Dr. André Blum. Edited and Revised by R. R. Tatlock. Illustrated by 128 full-page Photographic Plates, comprising about 350 examples of the finest Painting, Sculpture, Architecture, and Decorative Art of Early, Classic, Byzantine, Gothic, Renaissance, and Recent Times. Medium 8vo, gilt. 12s. 6d. net.

THE CHEAP COTTAGE AND SMALL HOUSE

By GORDON ALLEN, F.R.I.B.A. New Edition, remodelled and enlarged, containing over 150 Illustrations from Drawings and Photographs of Cottages and their Plans, Housing Schemes, etc., from typical Designs. Medium 8vo, cloth. 8s. 6d. net.

A BOOK OF BUNGALOWS AND MODERN HOMES

A series of Typical Designs and Plans. By CECIL J. H. KEELEY, F.S.I., A.R.San.I., Architect. Comprising 36 Designs, with large scale Plans, Brief Descriptions and Estimated Cost, including some two-Storey Houses, Frontispiece in colour, Interior Views, Photographic Plates, etc. Large 8vo, cloth, 7s. 6d. net.

MODERN THEATRES AND CINEMAS

By P. MORTON SHAND. A series of 80 plates giving over 100 examples of exteriors, interiors, foyers, vestibules, lighting, mural decoration, details, etc., of Theatres and Cinemas in the modern post-war style in France, Germany, England, Scandinavia, Italy, America, etc. Containing reproductions of the work of such architects as Margold, Kaufmann, Siclis, Gropius, Lipp, Ionides, Sauvage, de Soissons, Wilms, Mendelsohn, etc. Containing in addition numerous plans, elevations, sections in the text. Cr. 4to, art canvas. 15s. net.

BRITISH ARCHITECTS OF THE PRESENT DAY

By PROFESSOR C. H. REILLY, M.A., F.R.I.B.A., late Director of the Liverpool School of Architecture. An Account of Twelve Typical Figures, their Careers and Work, including Professor Adshead, Robert Atkinson, Sir Herbert Baker, Sir R. Blomfield, A. J. Davis, Sir E. Guy Dawber, Clough Williams-Ellis, W. Curtis Green, H. V. Lanchester, Sir E. L. Lutyens, Sir Giles Gilbert Scott and Walter Tapper. With 130 illustrations of well-known buildings, and including 12 portraits. Large 8vo, cloth. 7s. 6d. net.

ARCHITECTURAL DRAWING

By G. GORDON HAKE, F.R.I.B.A., and E. H. BUTTON, Architects. An Introductory Treatise for Architects and Students on work of every type and in every medium. With 96 pages, 16 pages of Half-tone Illustrations and 90 Line Illustrations. Cheaper reissue. 8vo, cloth. 7s. 6d. net.

GARDENS IN THE MAKING

By WALTER H. GODFREY. A simple Guide to the Planning of a Garden. With upwards of 70 Illustrations of Plans, Views, and various Garden Accessories. Crown 8vo, cloth. 7s. 6d. net.

THE ART AND CRAFT OF GARDEN MAKING

By THOMAS H. MAWSON, assisted by E. PRENTICE MAWSON, Fifth Edition, Revised and Enlarged. Containing 440 pages, illustrated by 544 Plans, Sketches and Photographs, and 5 colour Plates. Including Site, Entrances, Gates, Avenues, Terraces, Beds, Pergolas, Treillage, Rock and Water, Greenhouses, etc., etc., and list of Shrubs and Trees. Small folio, buckram, gilt. £3 15s. net.

SPANISH GARDENS

By Mrs. C. M. VILLIERS-STUART. With 6 plates in colour from the author's original water-colour drawings, 80 pages of reproductions of gardens, statuary, cascades, garden features, etc., from photographs, and numerous illustrations in the text from old engravings, pen drawings, etc. Small royal 8vo, cloth. 25s. net.

ENGLISH CHURCH SCREENS

A comprehensive Review of their Evolution and Design, including Great Roods, Tympana and Celures in Parish Churches during Medieval and Renaissance Times. By AYMER VALLANCE, M.A., F.S.A., author of "Crosses and Lychgates," "The Old Colleges of Oxford," etc. Illustrated by some 300 reproductions of typical examples, detail, carving, etc., from photographs, measured drawings and sketches, including many no longer extant and a series in colour from water-colour drawings. 4to, cloth. 25s. net.

OLD CROSSES AND LYCHGATES

A Study of their Design and Craftsmanship. By AYMER VALLANCE, M.A., F.S.A. With over 200 fine Illustrations from special Photographs, Old Prints, and Drawings. Crown 4to, art linen. 12s. 6d. net.

ENGLISH CHURCH WOODWORK AND FURNITURE

A Study in Craftsmanship from A.D. 1250-1550. By F. E. HOWARD and F. H. CROSSLEY, F.S.A. Illustrating, in over 480 examples from Photographs, the Development of Screens, Stalls, Benches, Font-Covers, Roofs, Doors, Porches, etc., with details of the Carved and Painted Decoration, etc., etc. Crown 4to, cloth, gilt. 25s. net.

ENGLISH CHURCH MONUMENTS, A.D. 1150-1550

By F. H. CROSSLEY, F.S.A. A survey of the work of the old English craftsmen in stone, marble, and alabaster. Containing over 250 pages, with upwards of 350 Illustrations, from special Photographs and Drawings. Crown 4to, cloth, gilt. 21s. net.

ENGLISH CHURCH FITTINGS AND FURNITURE

By the Rev. J. C. Cox, LL.D., F.S.A. A Popular Survey, treating of Churchyards, Bells, Fonts and Covers, Pulpits, Lecterns, Screens, Chained Books, Stained Glass, Organs, Plate and other features of interest. With upwards of 250 Illustrations from Photographs and Drawings. 8vo, cloth, gilt. 12s. 6d. net.

ANCIENT CHURCH CHESTS AND CHAIRS IN THE HOME COUNTIES ROUND GREATER LONDON

By FRED ROE, R.I., R.B.C. A survey of the finest of these survivals of ancient craftsmanship by the leading authority on the subject. With 95 illustrations, many full page, from drawings by the author and from photographs. Demy 4to, cloth, gilt. 12s. 6d. net.

OLD ENGLISH FURNITURE: THE OAK PERIOD, 1550-1630

Its Characteristics, Features, and Detail from Tudor Times to the Regency. By J. T. GARSIDE. Containing 30 plates reproduced from the author's drawings illustrating about 400 details of Table Legs; Bedposts; Corbels; Friezes; Capitals; Panels; Inlay Motives; Metal Fittings, etc. Including also drawings of type-pieces of the period and 20 photographic illustrations. With an Historical Introduction, etc. 8vo, cloth. 7s. 6d. net.

ENGLISH INTERIORS FROM SMALLER HOUSES OF THE XVIITH to XIXTH CENTURIES, 1660-1820

By M. JOURDAIN. Illustrating the simpler type of Design during the Stuart, Georgian, and Regency Periods. Containing 200 pages, and 100 Plates, comprising 200 Illustrations, from Photographs and Measured Drawings of Interiors, Chimney-pieces, Staircases, Doors, Ceilings, Panelling, Metalwork, Carving, etc. With descriptive text. 4to, cloth, gilt. 15s. net.

In 4 volumes forming an attractive Series of remarkable scope and completeness. Each volume has an extensive series of plates, and is a complete guide to the work of its Period. The volumes are remarkable for the beauty and number of their illustrations, the simplicity and clearness of their arrangement. The complete series is published at prices amounting to £10, but is supplied for the present at the special price of £9 net.

"These handsome volumes with their extremely fine and copious illustrations provide a full survey of English Furniture and Decoration."—*The Times.*

VOL. I. DECORATION AND FURNITURE IN ENGLAND DURING THE EARLY RENAISSANCE, 1500-1660

An Account of their Development and Characteristic Forms during the Tudor, Elizabethan and Jacobean Periods, by M. JOURDAIN. Containing about 300 pages, and over 200 full-page Plates (with Coloured Frontispiece and some in Photogravure), including over 400 Illustrations, from specially made Photographs and Measured Drawings, and from Engravings. Folio (size 14 x 10½ in.), cloth, gilt. £2 10s. net.

VOL. II. FURNITURE IN ENGLAND FROM 1066 TO 1760

By FRANCIS LENYGON. A Survey of the Development of its Chief Types. Containing 300 pages with over 400 Illustrations, from special Photographs, together with 5 in colour. Second Edition, revised with many new Illustrations. Folio (14 in. x 10½ in.), cloth, gilt. £2 10s. net.

VOL. III. DECORATION IN ENGLAND FROM 1640 TO 1770

By FRANCIS LENYGON. A Review of its Development and Features. Containing 300 pages with over 350 Illustrations, of which 133 are full-page, from special Photographs, and 4 in colour. Second Edition, Revised and Enlarged. Folio (14 in. x 10½ in.), cloth, gilt. £2 10s. net.

VOL. IV. DECORATION AND FURNITURE IN ENGLAND DURING THE LATER XVIIIth CENTURY, 1760-1820

An Account of their Development and Characteristic Forms, by M. JOURDAIN. Containing about 300 pages, with over 180 full-page Plates (a selection in Collotype), including over 400 Illustrations, from specially made Photographs and Measured Drawings, and from Engravings. Folio (size 14 x 10½ in.), cloth, gilt. £2 10s. net.

OLD ENGLISH FURNITURE FOR THE SMALL COLLECTOR: ITS HISTORY, TYPES AND SURROUNDINGS

By J. P. BLAKE and A. E. REVEIRS-HOPKINS. Containing 150 pages with about 130 illustrations from photographs, old prints and pictures, original designs, Ornaments, etc. The book is planned as a handy guide to the simpler types of old furniture which appeal to the collector of average means. Med. 8vo. 12s. 6d. net.

ENGLISH PLASTERWORK OF THE RENAISSANCE

By M. JOURDAIN. Comprising over 100 full-page plates of Elizabethan, Stuart, Georgian, and Adam ceilings, friezes, overmantels, panels, ornament, detail, etc., from specially taken photographs and from measured drawings and sketches. Demy 4to, cloth. 15s. net.

A HISTORY OF ENGLISH WALLPAPER

From the Earliest Period to 1914. By ALAN VICTOR SUGDEN and JOHN LUDLAM EDMONDSON. With 70 Plates in colour and 190 Illustrations, including many full-page Specimens of Wallpapers from the XVIth to the XXth Centuries. Large 4to, art buckram, gilt. £3 3s. net.

A Series of Handbooks written by experts, providing information of practical value to Connoisseurs, Collectors, Designers, and Students. Each volume forms an ideal introduction to its subject, and is fully illustrated by Reproductions in Colour and from Photographs. The following volumes are still available. 8vo, cloth, gilt, price 6s. net each.

OLD ENGLISH FURNITURE. By F. FENN and B. WYLLIE. With 94 Illustrations. *New Impression.*

OLD PEWTER. By MALCOLM BELL. With 106 Illustrations.

SHEFFIELD PLATE. By BERTIE WYLLIE. With 121 Illustrations.

FRENCH FURNITURE. By ANDRÉ SAGLIO. With 59 Illustrations.

DUTCH POTTERY AND PORCELAIN. By W. P. KNOWLES. With 54 Illustrations.

PORCELAIN. By WILLIAM BURTON. With 50 full-page Plates illustrating 87 examples from various Countries and Periods.

OLD PEWTER: ITS MAKERS AND MARKS

A Guide for Collectors, Connoisseurs, and Antiquaries. By HOWARD HERSCHEL COTTERELL, First Vice-President of the Society of Pewter Collectors. Containing about 500 pages, with 64 Plates of 200 Specimens of British Pewter, dated and described, and a List of 5,000 to 6,000 Pewterers, with Illustrations of their Touches and Secondary Marks, Facsimile Reproductions of existing Touch-Plates, and Text Illustrations. Cheaper reissue. Demy 4to, cloth, gilt. £3 3s. net.

OLD SILVER OF EUROPE AND AMERICA

From Early Times to the XIXth Century. By E. ALFRED JONES. A Survey of the Old Silver of England, America, Austria, Belgium, Canada, Czechoslovakia, Denmark, France, Germany, Holland, Hungary, Ireland, Italy, Norway, Poland, Portugal, Russia, Scotland, Spain, Sweden, Switzerland, etc. With a Chapter on Spurious Plate and 96 Photogravure Plates, comprising 537 subjects. Cheaper reissue. Crown 4to, art canvas, 18s. net.

CHINESE JADE

A COMPREHENSIVE INTRODUCTORY REVIEW FOR COLLECTORS AND STUDENTS. By STANLEY CHARLES NOTT. With an Introduction by SIR CECIL HARCOURT SMITH, K.C.V.O., formerly Director of the Victoria and Albert Museum. Dedicated by permission to Her Gracious Majesty Queen Mary. With a full series of illustrations of the finest products of the art of all periods on 40 plates in facsimile colour and 112 from photographs, including examples belonging to H.M. the King, H.M. Queen Mary, H.R.H. the Duke of Kent, and other English and Continental royal, private and public collections. Small 4to, cloth, gilt. £2 2s. net.

ORIENTAL LOWESTOFT

By J. A. LLOYD HYDE. Written with special reference to the trade with China and the porcelain decorated for the American market. Lavishly illustrated. £2 2s. net.

ENGLISH CONVERSATION PIECES

By SACHEVERELL SITWELL, author of "Southern Baroque," etc. A pictorial Survey of Domestic Portrait Groups and their Painters during the eighteenth and nineteenth centuries. With 6 Colour and 96 monochrome Plates illustrating the work of some 70 painters, famous and unknown, much of it before unpublished, and forming a vivid and attractive representation of contemporary social life and famous figures. With descriptive and historical notes. 4to, cloth, gilt. 21s. net.

No. I.—CHINESE ART

Including an Introduction by ROGER FRY and articles on Painting, Sculpture, Bronzes, Ceramics, Textiles, Jade, Enamels and Lacquer, etc., by LAURENCE BINYON, OSVALD SIREN, BERNARD RACKHAM, A. F. KENDRICK and W. W. WINKWORTH. With 23 fine full-page coloured plates, beautifully reproduced, of outstanding examples in public and private collections, and including also between 70 and 80 Photographic Illustrations on 52 plates, and a number of line cuts in the text, with maps, marks, tables of dynasties, etc. Large royal 8vo, cloth. 15s. net.

NO. II.—SPANISH ART

An Introductory Review of Architecture, Painting, Sculpture, Textiles, Ceramics, Woodwork, Metalwork, by ROYALL TYLER, SIR CHARLES HOLMES and H. ISHERWOOD KAY, GEOFFREY WEBB, A. F. KENDRICK, B. RACKHAM and A. VAN DE PUT, BERNARD BEVAN, and P. DE ARTINANO, respectively. With a General Introduction by R. R. TATLOCK, late Editor of *The Burlington Magazine*. Illustrated by 120 large scale reproductions of Paintings, Decorative Art, Buildings, etc., including 9 Plates in full colour, comprising 280 pictures in all. Royal 4to, cloth. 25s. net.

NO. III.—GEORGIAN ART

A Survey of Art in England during the reign of George III, 1760-1820, by leading authorities. The Sections comprise: *Painting* by J. B. MANSON; *Architecture and Sculpture* by GEOFFREY WEBB; *Ceramics* by BERNARD RACKHAM; *Woodwork* by OLIVER BRACKETT; *Textiles* by A. F. KENDRICK; *Minor Arts* by LOUISE GORDON-STABLES. With an Introduction by ROGER FRY. The Illustrations include 6 Plates in colour and 64 in half-tone, comprising some 100 subjects. Royal 4to, cloth. 21st. net.

THE DRAWINGS OF ANTOINE WATTEAU, 1684-1721

By Dr. K. T. PARKER, of the Ashmolean Museum, Oxford, Editor of "Old Master Drawings." A full, original and critical Survey. Illustrated by 100 Collotype Reproductions of selected characteristic Drawings from private and public collections, many unpublished, a Frontispiece in colour and 16 of the master's most important pictures. 4to, cloth, gilt. £2 2s. net.

A HISTORY OF BRITISH WATER-COLOUR PAINTING

By H. M. CUNDALL, F.S.A. With a Foreword by Sir H. HUGHES-STANTON, P.R.W.S. A New and Cheaper Edition, revised and enlarged, of this important standard work, with 64 full-page Illustrations in colour, and a full biographical list, arranged alphabetically, of the principal English Water-colourists. Large Medium 8vo, cloth. 15s. net.

HISTORIC TEXTILE FABRICS

By RICHARD GLAZIER. Containing: Materials—The Loom—Pattern—Tapestries—Dyed and Printed Fabrics—Church Vestments, etc., with about 100 Plates from Photographs and from the Author's Drawings including 4 in colour, and 43 Line Diagrams, illustrating over 200 varieties of Textile Design. Large 8vo, cloth, gilt. 21s. net.

THE ART AND CRAFT OF OLD LACE

In all Countries, from the XVIth to the Early XIXth Centuries. By ALFRED VON HENNEBERG. With an Introduction by WILHELM PINDER. Containing a full original account of the Development of Style and an Analysis of Technique and Texture. Illustrated by 190 full-page plates, 8 in colour, giving 60 specimens from scale diagrams and 250 of the finest pieces of Old Lace. Large 4to, cloth, gilt. £3 3s. net.

FURNITURE FOR SMALL HOUSES

By PERCY A. WELLS. Containing 56 Plates of Designs reproduced from Photographs and Working Drawings by the Author, together with Illustrations in the text. Cheaper reissue. Small 4to, cloth, 7s. 6d. net.

THE ART AND CRAFT OF HOME MAKING

By EDWARD W. GREGORY. Containing Practical Hints and Information on such subjects as Taking a House—Wallpapers—Furnishing Various Rooms —Pictures—Kitchen—Heating—Carpets—Curtains—Things that Get Out of Order, etc. Containing 224 pages, with 9 Plates in full colour of decorative schemes, numerous Photographs of Interiors, and many Sketches, Plans and Diagrams. Second Edition revised. Square 8vo, cloth. 7s. 6d. net.

THE NEW INTERIOR DECORATION

By DOROTHY TODD and RAYMOND MORTIMER. With over 200 Illustrations on 96 Plates of Interiors of every sort, Furniture, Carpets, Textiles, Lighting, Wall Painting, etc., of the new school by such Architects and Artists as Le Corbusier, Mallet-Stevens, Gropius, Oud, Duncan Grant, Lescaze, etc. With descriptive text. Demy 4to, art canvas. 12s. 6d. net.

MODERN DECORATIVE ART

A Series of 200 examples of Interior Decoration, Furniture, Lighting, Fittings, and other Ornamental Features. By MAURICE S. R. ADAMS. The book is arranged in sections, taking in turn each type of room, and giving its complete furnishing. Illustrated by 120 photographic plates and line drawings, with descriptive text. Demy 4to, art canvas, gilt. 8s. 6d. net.

DESIGN IN WOODWORK

By PERCY A. WELLS, author of "Modern Cabinetwork," etc. Illustrated by 25 full-page drawings comprising 150 diagrams and 47 plates from photographs of Mirrors, Stools, Clocks, Cabinets, Tables, Bookcases, etc. Demy 8vo, cloth. 6s. net.

HANDCRAFT IN WOOD AND METAL

A Handbook for the use of Teachers, Students, Craftsmen, and others. By JOHN HOOPER and ALFRED J. SHIRLEY. With over 300 Illustrations from Drawings and Photographs. Fifth Edition, revised and enlarged. Large 8vo, cloth. 10s. 6d. net.

CRAFTWORK IN METAL

A Practical Elementary Textbook for Teachers, Students, and Workers. By ALFRED J. SHIRLEY. Comprising a series of progressive Lessons and Exercises, illustrated by numerous full-page Plates from the Author's Drawings, each accompanied by detailed working directions, including also Practical Notes, Tables, etc. Medium 8vo, cloth. 5s. net.

BOOKCRAFTS AND BOOKBINDING. A Practical Course.

By JOHN MASON, Teacher at Leicester College of Arts and Crafts, etc., Containing sections on Historical Developments, various Binding Processes, Lettering, Leather, Paper, etc., with some 300 illustrations from diagrams and photographs of operations and finished designs. Large 8vo, cloth. 8s. 6d. net.

PRACTICAL CRAFTWORK DESIGN

A SERIES OF progressive LESSONS AND EXAMPLES IN LEATHERWORK GLOVE-MAKING, RAFFIA, AND FRETWORK. By WINIFRED CLARKE, Teacher of Needlework and Leather at Loughborough College. With numerous plates in colour, half-tone and line from the author's designs, and from photographs of finished objects. Royal 8vo. Half-cloth. 7s. 6d. net.

COLOUR: A MANUAL OF ITS STUDY AND PRACTICE

By H. BARRETT CARPENTER, late Headmaster of the School of Art, Rochdale. A Series of 16 concise but very practical chapters, based on the Author's experiments, on Harmony—Contrast—Discord—Keynotes—Intermingling—Effect of Lighting—Dirty Colour—Black-and-White, etc. Illustrated by 24 Plates (some double size), printed in colour; giving 40 Examples of Colour Combinations, Grading, Toning, etc., including some new examples in colour of application in Historic Design. New and Revised Impression. 8vo, cloth, gilt. 9s. net.

A COLOUR CHART

Issued in connection with the above book. Consisting of a circle 17 inches in diameter, printed in Graded Colour, showing 14 shades, Combinations and Contrasts. With explanatory letterpress. Folio, stout paper. 2s. 6d. net.

ALPHABETS, OLD AND NEW

With 224 complete Alphabets, 30 series of Numerals, many Ancient Dates, etc. Selected and Arranged by LEWIS F. DAY. With a short account of the Development of the Alphabet. Crown 8vo, cloth. 5s. net.

PEN PRACTICE

By WALTER HIGGINS. Chapters on Tools, Broad-pen Practice, Spacing, Italics, Uncials and Half-uncials, Setting out, A Cursive Hand, etc. With 27 Plates specially drawn by the Author, giving some hundreds of Letters, Ornaments and Exercises, and 6 from selected Historical Examples. Second Edition, revised. Crown 8vo, paper covers, 1s. 6d. net; or boards 2s. 6d. net.

THE ROMAN ALPHABET AND ITS DERIVATIVES

A large-sized Reproduction of the Alphabet of the Trajan Column. By ALLEN W. SEABY. A Series of large Plates, printed from the wood blocks, and including typical examples of Renaissance, Gothic, and Modern Alphabets and Types. With Introduction and descriptive Notes. Medium 4to half-bound, or in portfolio. 4s. 6d. net.

101 THINGS FOR LITTLE FOLKS TO DO

By A. C. HORTH, Editor of "Educational Handcraft," Examiner to the Board of Education, and author of numerous craftwork manuals. Containing sections on paper folding, cutting and making, and making many amusing and useful objects, painting, etc. With 90 full page practical diagrams by the author and a special series of 31 plates from designs in colour. An unfailing source of entertainment and instruction for young children of both sexes. Crown 8vo, cloth. 5s. net.

101 THINGS FOR GIRLS TO DO

By A. C. HORTH, Editor of "Educational Handwork," etc. With practical sections on Stitchery, the making of decorative Household Articles in felt, leather, gesso, raffia, Hints on Mending, Cleaning, First-Aid, etc. Illustrated by numerous Line Diagrams, Photographs of finished objects, etc. Crown 8vo, cloth. 5s. net.

101 THINGS FOR A BOY TO MAKE

By A. C. HORTH. With Notes on Workshop Practice and Processes, Tools, Joints, and full reliable directions for making Working Models. Illustrated by numerous full-page and smaller practical Diagrams and Sketches specially prepared. Second Edition, revised and enlarged. Crown 8vo, cloth. 5s. net.

ART IN DAILY LIFE FOR YOUNG AND OLD

By D. D. SAWER, late Art Lecturer at the Diocesan College, Brighton. A companion and complement to the following work with a Foreword by P. H. JOWETT, A.R.C.A. A comprehensive course for Teachers, Students and Art Lovers; treating of the Place of Drawing, Plants and their Use, Figure Drawing and Drapery, Animal Drawing, Modelling Shapes and Figures, Casting, Clay Modelling, Object Drawing, Notes on Crafts, Composition, Design, applied and graphic. With 10 plates in colour and 200 illustrations in line and half-tone. Medium 8vo, cloth. 10s. 6d. net.

EVERYDAY ART AT SCHOOL AND HOME

By D. D. SAWER. With an appreciative Foreword by Sir Michael Sadler, C.B., Oxford. A Practical Course based on the new Board of Education "Suggestions to Teachers," and adaptable to Dalton Methods, containing graduated lessons on Design, Flower-painting, etc., with sections on Architectural Drawing, Lettering, Stained Glass, Leatherwork, and other Crafts. With 64 Plates in half-tone, from the Author's Drawings, numerous full-page and smaller Line Illustrations, and 8 Plates in colour. Second Edition, revised and enlarged. Medium 8vo, cloth. 10s. 6d. net.

PERSPECTIVE IN DRAWING

A simple Introductory Account. By D. D. SAWER. With an Introduction by Professor ALLEN W. SEABY, late Professor of Fine Art, University of Reading. With Sections on Basic Principles, the Cube, Cylinder, Shadows, Reflections, Aerial Perspective, Colour and Drawing. Illustrated by over 100 Diagrams and Sketches, a Frontispiece in colour, and reproductions from Photographs. Crown 8vo, cloth. 5s. net.

SKETCHING AND PAINTING FOR YOUNG AND OLD

An Elementary Practical Manual. By D. D. SAWER, with a Foreword by LORD BADEN-POWELL. With chapters on: Ungathered Wealth, a Day Out, Materials, Practice, the First Sketch Out of Doors, Composition, Mounting and Framing. Illustrated by a coloured Frontispiece, 8 plates in line and half-tone, and 31 text illustrations from the author's sketches, diagrams, etc. Crown 8vo, stiff covers, 1s. 6d. net; or quarter-cloth, 2s. net.

LAUGHS AND SMILES and How to Draw Them. By A. A. Braun, author of "Figures, Faces and Folds" and other works.

Containing 45 Plates, printed in tints, of numerous constructional sketches, building up in successive stages humorous likenesses of well-known personages. Comprising about 300 sketches, with concise text and anatomical diagrams. Oblong 4to, decorative boards, cloth back. 3s. 6d. net.

FIGURES, FACES AND FOLDS

For Fashion Artists, Dress Designers, and Art Students. By ADOLPHE ARMAND BRAUN. Containing 112 comparative Plates, giving over 300 Illustrations of Costume and Drapery. Including a special series of nude and draped studies from models specially posed for fashion work. With practical text, Dress diagrams, Figure details, Anatomy analysis, etc. Cheaper reissue. Demy 4to, stiff paper covers, 10s. 6d. net; cloth, gilt, 12s. 6d. net.

THE CHILD IN ART AND NATURE

By A. A. BRAUN. Containing chapters on Anatomy, Development, and Expression, and over 300 Illustrations from Photographs and Drawings of child poses, expressions, the Child Figure in Art. Second Edition. 4to, in stiff covers, 10s. 6d. net; or cloth, gilt, 12s. 6d. net.

A MANUAL OF HISTORIC ORNAMENT

Being an Account of the Development of Architecture and the Historic Arts, for the use of Students and Craftsmen. By RICHARD GLAZIER, A.R.I.B.A. Fifth Edition, revised and enlarged. Containing 700 Illustrations, chiefly from the Author's Pen Drawings, including many new to this Edition from various sources, and a special series of coloured and Photographic Plates of Ornament of the Orient and the Renaissance. Large 8vo. cloth. 12s. 6d. net.

A HANDBOOK OF ORNAMENT

By Professor F. SALES MEYER. With 3,000 Illustrations of the Elements and the Application of Decoration to Objects, e.g. Vases, Frets, Diapers, Consoles, Frames, Jewellery, Heraldry, etc., grouped on over 300 Plates, reproduced from the Author's specially prepared Drawings. With descriptive text to each subject. Large 8vo, cloth. 15s. net.

THE STYLES OF ORNAMENT

From Prehistoric Times to the Middle of the XIXth Century. A Series of 3,500 Examples Arranged in Historical Order, with descriptive text. By ALEXANDER SPELTZ. Revised and Edited by R. PHENÉ SPIERS, F.S.A., F.R.I.B.A. Containing 560 pages, with 400 full-page Plates exhibiting upwards of 3,500 separate Illustrations. Large 8vo, cloth, gilt. 15s. net.

ABSTRACT DESIGN

A Practical Manual on the Making of Pattern. By AMOR FENN, late Head of the Art Section, Goldsmith's College, New Cross. A series of careful, informative sections on Conditions, Elements, etc. Illustrated by about 180 full-page Designs from the Author's specially-prepared Drawings. 8vo, cloth, 12s. 6d. net.

PATTERN DESIGN

For Students, treating in a practical way the Anatomy, Planning, and Evolution of Repeated Ornament. By LEWIS F. DAY. Containing about 300 pages, and 300 practical Illustrations from specially prepared Drawings and Photographs of the Principles of Repeat Design, the "Drop," the "Spot" Geometrical Ornament, etc. New edition, revised and enlarged by AMOR FENN, with many fresh Illustrations, including a series in colour. Demy 8vo, cloth, gilt. 10s. 6d. net.

NATURE AND ORNAMENT

By LEWIS F. DAY. NATURE THE RAW MATERIAL OF DESIGN, treating chiefly of the decorative possibilities of Plant Form, its growth, features, and detail. With 350 Illustrations, chiefly grouped comparatively under Flowers, Seed Vessels, Fruits, Berries, etc., specially drawn by Miss J. FOORD. New and cheaper Edition, revised, with a Chapter by MARY HOGARTH. Demy 8vo, cloth. 5s. net.

DRAWING, DESIGN AND CRAFTWORK

For Teachers, Students, and Designers. By FREDK. J. GLASS. Containing 262 pages, with some 2,000 Illustrations on 156 Plates, from Drawings by the Author and others, and Historic Designs: Chinese, Persian, Japanese, Medieval, etc. Third Edition revised and enlarged with many new Plates, including a special series in colour of Historic and Modern Designs. Demy 8vo, cloth. 12s. net.

APPLIED ART

A Course of Study in Drawing, Painting, Design and Handicraft, arranged for the self-instruction of Teachers, Parents and Students. By P. J. LEMOS, Editor of *The School Arts Magazine*. Containing 400 pages lavishly illustrated by 37 Plates in colour and 246 in line, pencil, wash and half-tone, from specially-prepared drawings and photographs, comprising a total of over 3,000 illustrations. Large 8vo, cloth, gilt. 28s. net.

A study of this attractive work will stimulate young and old to appreciate the beauty of nature, to learn to picture her messages and to woo harmonies from her storehouse of line, form, pattern and colour that will beautify and influence the whole of their everyday life. To teachers, who, as often happens, are called upon to impart instruction in arts and crafts along with other subjects, it should prove invaluable.

THE ART TEACHER

By P. J. LEMOS, Director of the Museum of Fine Arts, Leland Stanford Junior University, and Editor of *The School Arts Magazine*. A comprehensive compendium of Art Teaching Ideas, Suggestions and Methods based upon the practice of leading schools and colleges in the United States and other countries. Containing 500 pages, profusely illustrated by 68 Plates in colour and about 1,000 illustrations in line, pencil and wash from the author's specially-prepared drawings, together with photographs. Large 8vo, cloth. £2 net.

This unique work is of outstanding importance and value. It provides a carefully graded and correlated course of art education, comprising Drawing, Painting Design, Colour Work, Paper Work, Modelling, Pottery, Lettering, Toys and Woodwork, Sewing, Weaving, Basketry, Arts and Crafts exemplified in Home and Garden, Puppets, Stagecraft, Picture and Nature Study, etc.

MODELLING

By F. J. GLASS. Containing Chapters on Figure Modelling; Relief Work; Composition; Casting; Gelatine Moulding; etc. With a section on History and Ornament. Illustrated by about 30 Plates of stages and processes, 35 Plates of Sculpture and many Line Illustrations. Royal 8vo, cloth, gilt. 15s. net.

THE ART AND CRAFT OF LINO CUTTING AND PRINTING

By CLAUDE FLIGHT, author of "Tinker, Tailor," etc. With a Foreword by J. E. BARTON. Treating of Designing, Cutting, Printing, Alterations, etc. With 77 Illustrations, largely full-page, including 5 in full colour, by the author and others, and also diagrams and prints in various stages. Tall 8vo, decorative boards. 3s. 6d. net.

PRACTICAL WOODCARVING

By ELEANOR ROWE. Third Edition, revised and enlarged, in Two Parts; I. ELEMENTARY WOODCARVING, embodying "Hints on Woodcarving." With numerous Illustrations, many full-page, from Drawings and Photographs of carving operations, examples and details. II. ADVANCED WOODCARVING. With numerous Illustrations, many full-page from Drawings and Photographs of historic and modern carvings. Demy 8vo, limp cloth, lettered, 5s. net each; or two parts in one volume, cloth, gilt, 10s. net.

SAMPLERS AND STITCHES

A Handbook of the Embroiderer's Art. By MRS. ARCHIBALD CHRISTIE. Containing 40 full-page Reproductions from Photographs, a Frontispiece in colour, and 289 Text Drawings. Third Edition, revised and enlarged. Crown 4to, boards, canvas back. 25s. net.

ART IN NEEDLEWORK

A BOOK ABOUT EMBROIDERY. By LEWIS F. DAY and MARY BUCKLE. Fourth Edition, revised by MARY HOGARTH. Including a specially worked Series of Stitch-Samplers, numerous supplementary Diagrams and many Plates of Historic Embroidery—Chinese, Medieval, Italian, French and Modern English. With additional Examples of Modern Work by DUNCAN GRANT, MRS. NEWALL, MRS. STOLL, D. HAGER, and others. Containing 280 pages, 80 full-page Plates, reproduced from Photographs, and 50 Illustrations in the text. Crown 8vo, cloth. 7s. 6d. net.

STITCH PATTERNS AND DESIGNS FOR EMBROIDERY

By ANNE BRANDON-JONES. Containing 48 pages with 45 photographic examples on 12 Plates of simple and effective embroidery Motives, a Frontispiece in colour and numerous Text Illustrations of Stitches and Methods. Crown 4to, paper wrappers, 3s. net; or in cloth, 4s. net.

CANVAS EMBROIDERY

A Manual for Students and Amateurs by LOUISA F. PESEL. Containing 48 pages of text, a coloured Frontispiece, and 14 specially prepared Plates showing Stitches and methods. Medium oblong 4to, paper wrappers, 3s. net; or bound in cloth, 4s. net.

ENGLISH EMBROIDERY. I. DOUBLE-RUNNING, OR BACK-STITCH

By LOUISA F. PESEL. With coloured Frontispiece, 10 specially drawn Plates of 45 Working Designs, and 8 Plates from Photographs of 10 English and Coptic Samplers, comprising numerous Patterns and Motives. With Practical Text and a Preface by ETTA CAMPBELL, Embroidery Teacher, Winchester School of Arts. Uniform with "Canvas Embroidery." Large oblong 4to, paper wrappers, 3s. net; or boards, cloth back, 4s. net.

ENGLISH EMBROIDERY. II. CROSS-STITCH

By LOUISA F. PESEL. With a Coloured Frontispiece, 10 specially drawn Plates of 32 Working Designs, etc., and 8 Plates from Photographs of 15 typical English Samplers and Objects. Comprising 43 subjects, giving hundreds of Patterns and Motives. With Practical Text and a Preface by Professor R. GLEADOWE, late Slade Professor of Fine Arts, Oxford University. Large oblong 4to, paper wrappers, 3s. net; or boards, cloth back, 4s. net.

ILLUSTRATED STITCHERY DECORATIONS

By WINIFRED M. CLARKE. Containing 19 Plates from the Author's specially prepared Drawings, giving some 120 useful original Motives: Borders, Rosettes, Floral Elements, Patterns, Lettering and Worked Objects, such as Bags, Blotters, etc. Including a coloured Frontispiece, Introductory Text and full descriptive Notes on the Plates. Crown 4to, stiff paper wrappers, 3s. net; boards, cloth back, 4s. net.

MODERN DESIGN IN EMBROIDERY

By REBECCA CROMPTON, Examiner and Occasional Inspector in Women's Crafts to the Board of Education. Edited by DAVIDE C. MINTER. A novel approach to the craft on modern lines. With chapters on Creative Embroidery, the Value of Line, Fillings, Tone Value, Colour, etc. Illustrated by 4 Plates in colour, 74 Photographs of finished samplers, all specially designed and worked by the author, and 112 practical Line Diagrams in the text. Large 8vo, cloth, 8s. 6d. net.

COMPOSITION

An Analysis of the Principles of Pictorial Design. By CYRIL C. PEARCE, R.B.A. With chapters on Tone, Distribution, Gradation, Scale, Perspective, Rhythm, Harmony and Balance of Colour, Discords. Illustrated by 130 sketches and diagrams, 6 plates in colour, and 28 full-page illustrations from great masters. Med. 8vo. 10s. 6d. net.

ANIMAL ANATOMY AND DRAWING

By EDWIN NOBLE. Illustrated by a series of Plates in facsimile of the Author's Drawings of HORSES, CATTLE, DOGS, BIRDS and WILD ANIMALS, representing also Features, Details, etc. Including also numerous full-page and smaller line drawings of Muscles, Bones, etc. Med. 8vo. 10s. 6d. net.

PEN DRAWING

A Practical Manual on Materials, Technique, Style, Texture, etc. By G. M. ELLWOOD. Containing sections on History—Technique—Materials—Figures, Faces and Hands—Style and Methods—Landscape and Architecture—Modern Work—Magazine Illustration—Humorous Drawing Advertisements—Fashion. With 100 pages of illustrations by the chief pen draughtsmen of present and recent times. Med. 8vo. 10s. 6d. net.

THE ART AND PRACTICE OF SKETCHING

A Comprehensive Treatise on the Practice of Sketching by every method. By JASPER SALWEY, A.R.I.B.A. The Author deals successively with various media—Pen, Pencil, Water-colour, Oil, Wash, Crayon, Chalk, etc., and gives a complete account of the Technique of each. Illustrated by 64 plates of half-tone illustration and 6 plates in colour, from the work of great artists. Med. 8vo. 10s. 6d. net.

THE ART OF DRAWING IN LEAD PENCIL

By JASPER SALWEY, A.R.I.B.A. A Practical Manual dealing with Materials, Technique, Notes and Sketching, Building up, Form and Style, Process Reproduction, etc. Second Edition, revised and enlarged. Containing 232 pages with 122 reproductions of selected pencil drawings of Land and Seascapes, Figure-Studies, Book-Illustrations, etc. Med. 8vo. 10s. 6d. net.

SKETCHING IN LEAD PENCIL

By JASPER SALWEY, A.R.I.B.A. An Introduction to the same author's "Art of Drawing in Lead Pencil," but dealing entirely with sketching as differentiated from the making of finished Drawings. A practical manual for the Architect, Student and Artist. Containing 111 pages and 56 Illustrations, by well-known artists in the medium, and by the author. 7s. 6d. net.

SKETCHING FROM NATURE

A Practical Treatise on the Principles of Pictorial Composition. By F. J. GLASS. CONTENTS: Choice of Subject and Planning of Sketch—Tones—Exercise in Composition—Examples from the Old Masters. With 6 Plates in colour, numerous compositions from the Author's Drawings, and a series by past masters of Landscape Painting. Med. 8vo. 10s. 6d. net.

DRAWING FOR ART STUDENTS AND ILLUSTRATORS

By ALLEN W. SEABY. Containing 220 pages, with 133 Illustrations printed in Sepia, mostly full-page Plates, from Drawings by Old and Modern Artists. Second Edition, revised and enlarged. 8vo, cloth. 10s. 6d. net.

27

FASHION DRAWING AND DESIGN

By LOUIE E. CHADWICK. Illustrated by numerous examples of Historic Fashion Plates, Explanatory Sketches by the Author, Figure Studies, and a series of about 80 full-page and double Plates of Contemporary Fashion Drawings by well-known artists. Large 8vo, cloth. 7s. 6d. net.

THE ART OF THE BODY

Rhythmic Exercises for Health and Beauty. By MARGUERITE AGNIEL, Dancer and Physical Instructress. A series of simple, easy and enjoyable exercises, illustrated by numerous Photographic Plates, specially posed by the Author. With 100 subjects on 64 Plates, including many reproductions of dance poses and figure studies, draped and nude. CONTENTS: Functions of the Spine—How to Walk Well—Figure Reducing—Exercises for the Digestive Organs—Back and Neck—Legs and Ankles—The Care of the Hands and Feet—Skin, Eyes and Teeth—Constipation—Women's Disorders, etc. Large 8vo, cloth, gilt. 12s. 6d. net.

LIVING SCULPTURE

A Record of Expression in the Human Figure. By BERTRAM PARK and YVONNE GREGORY. With an historical and descriptive Introduction by G. MONTAGUE ELLWOOD. Comprising a Series of 47 full-page Studies of Selected Male and Female Figures with descriptive Notes. Small 4to, cloth, gilt. 12s. 6d. net.

ROUND THE WORLD IN FOLK TALES

A Regional Treatment. By RACHEL M. FLEMING. 16 Tales from Iceland, Mexico, Africa, Australia, etc., told in a fresh, easy style. With 17 illustrations from drawings and photographs. 8vo, boards 2s. net; cloth, 3s. net.

DINNER BUILDING

A Book of entertaining and practical instruction in the Noble Arts of Cooking and Eating. Written by W. TEIGNMOUTH SHORE. With an Introduction by GILBERT FRANKAU. A series of 42 bright, stimulating but practical Talks on such subjects as The Perfect Dinner, Sandwichery, Remnant Days, Cabbages and Things, incorporating hundreds of fresh recipes of all kinds. Cheaper reissue. F'cap 8vo, cloth, lettered. 2s. net.

THE "SHELL" GUIDES TO THE COUNTIES OF ENGLAND

Each containing from 50 to 60 pages, illustrated mainly by photographs, with map. 4to, in flexible binding. 2s. 6d. net each.

Volumes ready include:
CORNWALL; DERBYSHIRE; DEVON; DORSET; KENT; SOMERSET; and WILTSHIRE.

To appear shortly:
BUCKINGHAMSHIRE; HAMPSHIRE; NORTHUMBERLAND and DURHAM (in one volume).

BATSFORD'S PICTORIAL GUIDES TO EUROPEAN CITIES

I. STOCKHOLM. II. COPENHAGEN. III. AMSTERDAM. IV. HAMBURG.

Their Layout, Highways, Byways and Waterways, Distinctive Buildings, Life, Work and Play, presented in a series of some 100 attractive modern photographs, specially taken by Geoffrey Gilbert. With Tourist information and full informative captions. Square 8vo, in stiff covers. 2s. 6d. net per volume.

CIRCUS PARADE

By JOHN S. CLARKE, Ex-Lion Tamer. A graphic first-hand survey and pictorial review of its fascination and thrills as seen in the acts and performers, with some account of the history of its past. Illustrated by some 120 vivid Photographs and Old Prints, and a Frontispiece in colour. Demy 8vo, cloth, with decorative photographic jacket. 7s. 6d. net.

MOTOR RACING AND RECORD BREAKING

By the well-known Record-holding Racer, CAPTAIN G. E. EYSTON, Author of "Flat Out," etc., and BARRÉ LYNDON, Author of "Circuit Dust," etc. An historical account of achievements and thrills in many countries, and the influence of racing on car design. With 110 vivid Photographic Illustrations of track and road racing in Europe and America, hill-climbing, risks and personalities, etc. Including a colour Frontispiece. Demy 8vo. 7s. 6d. net.

THE WAR OF THE GUNS

Experiences of a Battery Signaller on the Climax of the Western Front, 1917-19. By AUBREY WADE. With an Introduction by EDMUND BLUNDEN, Author of "Undertones of War," etc. A graphic and vividly written first-hand account of the last desperate fighting round Ypres, Messines, Passchendaele, the Cambrai front, the German break-through, Villers-Bretonneux, and the final advance. Illustrated by some 120 fine photographs, English and German, of trench fighting, artillery work, etc. With a coloured Frontispiece by SIR WILLIAM ORPEN, R.A. Demy 8vo. 7s. 6d. net.

Forthcoming additions to the "NEW CENTURY" LIBRARY include the following:

VICTORIAN PANORAMA.. By PETER QUENNELL.

The life of Victorian England illustrated from photographs. 7s. 6d. net.

TO THE MOVIES. By GILBERT SELDES. 7s. 6d. net.

THE R.M.S. QUEEN MARY

A Picture Record of the great Steamship, 1930-1936. From Photographs by STEWART BALE and others. With Introduction and descriptive notes by GEORGE BLAKE, author of "The Shipbuilders," etc. With fine views of construction, trials, machinery, saloons, cabins, fittings, etc. Square 8vo, 4to cloth, pictorial sides, 2s. 6d. net; or full leather gilt, 5s. net.

THE BOOK OF SPEED

With 165 superb Illustrations in photogravure. Including: The Quest of Speed by STEPHEN KING-HALL; The Dawn of Flight by Col. ETHERTON; Speed in the Air by G. DE HAVILAND; "400 Miles an Hour!" by Flight-Lt. G. H. STAINFORTH; Motor Record Breaking by G. E. T. EYSTON; "What It Feels Like!" by Sir MALCOM CAMPBELL; Speed-Boats by H. SCOTT-PAINE; Motor-Cycle Racing by JAMES GUTHRIE; Speed by Rail by CECIL J. ALLEN :The Ocean Routes by Sir A. ROSTRON; Speed in Warfare by Maj.-Gen. FULLER. 4to, cloth. 5s. net.

SPEED ON SALT

By GEORGE EYSTON and W. F. BRADLEY. With a Foreword by SIR MALCOLM CAMPBELL. A graphic first-hand review of their pioneer record-breaking motor-runs on the Bonneville Salt Flats, Utah, U.S.A., including the world's land speed record of 300 m.p.h., and the world's 24-hour record. With 132 attractive illustrations from special photographs of machines and men. Frontispiece in colour and coloured jacket by BRIAN COOK. 4to, cloth. 5s. net.

ROYAL PROGRESS: ONE HUNDRED YEARS OF BRITISH MONARCHY, 1837-1937

By HECTOR BOLITHO. A fascinating account of the domestic history of the British Royal Family from the accession of Queen Victoria in 1837 to the Coronation of George VI in 1937. Profusely illustrated from old paintings and prints, and old and modern photographs, together with six plates in colour. Demy 8vo, cloth. 7s. 6d. net.

FARMING ENGLAND

By A. G. STREET. A broad general survey of English agriculture which will enable the ordinary man to look at the countryside with a new eye, to compare the farming of one region with that of another, and enjoy the fine old rural architecture of the farmhouses, and the age-old traditions they carry on, often side by side with new scientific methods. Copiously illustrated with fine, modern photographs of types and methods of farming in every English region, with a Frontispiece in colour. Demy 8vo. 7s. 6d. net.

A Companion Volume to "The Spirit of London"

THE SPIRIT OF PARIS

By PAUL COHEN-PORTHEIM. This is one of the last works completed by the author before his lamented death. No one had a better eye for a city than Paul Cohen-Portheim, and in this book he has contrived one of the most delightful "portraits of places" he attempted—one that not only describes the architectural background, but gives a real insight into the lives, work, pleasures and activities of Parisians of every type. It is delightfully illustrated by over 120 Photographs. Demy 8vo, cloth. 7s. 6d. net.

Uniform with "English Conversation Pieces"

FRENCH PAINTING IN THE XIXTH CENTURY

By JAMES LAVER. Containing 12 Plates in colour and 96 in monochrome, with Notes on painters and pictures by MICHAEL SEVIER, and a Postcript by ALFRED FLECHTHEIM. Both for its scholarship and illustration this book should form one of the finest and most definitive ever devoted to its great subject. The pictures illustrated are nearly all taken from private collections, either English, Continental or American. Crown 4to, Cloth gilt. 21s. net.

ART AND UNDERSTANDING

By MARGARET H. BULLEY (M. H. Armitage), Lecturer and Examiner on Art, author of "Art and Counterfeit," etc. A comparative survey of the ideas underlying art, old and modern, pictorial and decorative, true and false, contrasting achievements and failures, &c. With 20 chapters on (*inter alia*) Psychology, Technique, Function, Form, etc.; full comments on the Illustrations; and a miniature anthology of striking quotations, prose and verse. Including 275 Illustrations of paintings, drawings, architecture, decorative objects, etc., from the work of primitive races, children, and masters old and new. Large 8vo, cloth. 15s. net.

ENGLISH QUILTING, OLD AND NEW

A CONCISE REVIEW by ELIZABETH HAKE. With an Historical Account and Practical Directions for working. Illustrated from numerous Diagrams of Patterns and Tools, and some 50 photographs of selected examples from Devon and Somerset, Wales, Durham, and abroad, and of present-day working. 4to boards, 5s. 6d. net; cloth, 6s. 6d. net.

INDEX TO AUTHORS' NAMES AND SERIES

Printed in Great Britain by The Stanhope Press Ltd., Rochester, Kent.